Corporate Travel
Hiding in Plain Sight
Workbook

Claudia Unger

D1408789

Editorial & Design Services: The Write Factor
www.thewritefactor.co.uk

Corporate Travel
Hiding in Plain Sight
Workbook

Corporate Travel
Hiding in Plain Sight
Workbook

Claudia Unger

Table of Contents

Corporate Travel: Past, Present, and Future   49

Who is Who in Corporate Travel   83

Foreword

This workbook complements the book *Corporate Travel: Hiding in Plain Sight*. It aims to walk you through the five key areas already discussed in the book. But rather than 'just' reading information I invite you to think, search, find and build up your own opinions on the topics raised.

When I started lecturing, the first thing I said to my students was: "You shouldn't believe everything you read online, nor should you believe everything you read in a book, and for that matter you shouldn't even believe everything I say". Today's world is changing at rapid speed and there are constantly new products, services, thoughts and books emerging on various topics. So always take everything with a pinch of salt – and make up your own mind.

The information, questions and tasks provided in this book are designed to help you form an opinion about corporate travel in general, and the various topics in particular. Note that what I'm providing here is just a tiny window into a much larger world. You could spend hours upon hours on just one of the topics presented here – and you're welcome to do just that.

The structure of this workbook is straight forward: there are five parts overall featuring a travel related quote, checklist of what you'll be able to do or know after completing the exercises, an introduction to the general topic and a list of handy key facts at the end. That's the basic framework.

Within the parts, the subtopics are discussed following an equally simple structure: a little introduction is followed by some critical thinking questions. You'll then be asked to do some desk research – mostly online – to further your knowledge and are prompted with a question to 'test' what you've found out. Lastly, you'll be presented with a short case study on a particular industry challenge. Some questions prompt an analysis of the information and you're invited to argue your opinion.

As also mentioned in *Corporate Travel: Hiding in Plain Sight,* this workbook doesn't claim to offer a full view across everything in the industry. It's merely a starting point to look at this sector and see it for what it is: an economic powerhouse driving international relations.

Should you wish to discuss any of the exercises or would like my opinion, please stop by my website **www.c-asinunger.com** or look for *C – as in Unger* on Facebook. I'd be very happy to know how you got on, what you liked and what you didn't, and which topics you'd like to see covered in the next edition.

With love and thanks,

Claudia Unger

CORPORATE TRAVEL:
Part of the Big Picture

Travel is fatal to prejudice, bigotry, and narrow-mindedness.
~ *Mark Twain*

Checklist

By the end of this part you'll be able to:

✓ Define tourism in your own words.

✓ Define corporate travel and how important it is to the global economy.

✓ Know about different forms of meetings and reasons for travel.

✓ Explain the role of virtual meetings and their impact on corporate travel.

Introduction

Tourism: we immediately think of sunbathing on beaches, surfing waves or skiing mountains. Recreation, relaxation and faraway places. And as nice as that is, there's another side to tourism: economics. Travel and tourism are an important contributor to national GDPs (gross domestic product), accounting for about 9% (direct, indirect and induced) globally.

This first part of the workbook engages you with the big picture of tourism, as well as its business travel components, the latter having a significant global impact on the economy (about 1/3 of overall tourism spending), though one that is much less known.

To set the scene, let's define tourism and think about this industry as a whole. The research exercise and case study will raise your awareness of tourism as a vital source of income for regions, countries, and communities.

Corporate travel is part of the wider business travel industry, which mainly includes the so-called MICE sector (meetings, incentives, conferences and events). Again we'll look at the differences between the sectors, but also how they might benefit from one another. The case study about integrating meetings and corporate travel will be of particular interest.

Lastly, there's another form of meeting that's gaining traction in the corporate travel industry: going virtual. There are fully virtual conferences now available, and, although that's not the norm, it's certainly something to think about as a possible alternative for actual – that is physical – travel.

The Big Picture: Tourism

The importance of tourism for the global economy is proven beyond doubt. Organisations like the World Tourism Organisation (WTO) and the World Travel & Tourism Council (WTTC) are at the forefront of promoting its importance as well as educating the public of its possibilities.

Critical Thinking

The following three questions should be fairly easy to answer, but if you need help, have a look at Chapter One of the book *Corporate Travel: Hiding in Plain Sight*.

(1) What is tourism?

In your own words, describe what tourism is. What are the main components?

_____

_____

_____

_____

_____

_____

_____

_____

_____

_____

_____

_____

_____

(2) How does tourism relate to globalisation?

Look back at Mark Twain's quote at the beginning of this part. How do you think this applies to tourism? And how does it fit in with globalisation and a world 'without borders'?

_____

_____

_____

_____

_____

_____

_____

_____

_____

_____

_____

_____

_____

_____

_____

_____

_____

_____

_____

(3) What's the economic importance of tourism?

How important do you think tourism is for the world? How many people are employed in this industry? What do they do? Jot down some thoughts here before moving on to the research exercise on the next page.

_____

_____

_____

_____

_____

_____

_____

_____

_____

_____

_____

_____

_____

_____

_____

_____

_____

_____

Research

You've been thinking a lot about tourism and economics. You might have read the first chapter of Corporate Travel: Hiding in Plain Sight to deepen your understanding. Now it's time for some practical research. Note that you'll very likely encounter some research during your career so consider this as practice.

Go online to the pages of the United Nation's World Tourism Organization (WTO). Find their latest edition of the Tourism Highlights report. While reading this, consider the following questions:

(1) What has changed from the figures used in *Corporate Travel: Hiding in Plain Sight?*

(2) Are there any aspects you hadn't considered in the earlier exercises?

_____

_____

_____

_____

_____

_____

_____

_____

_____

_____

_____

_____

_____

_____

_____

_____

_____

_____

_____

After reading, consider and answer this question:

(3) Knowing the figures, has your view towards tourism changed? In what way?

_____

_____

_____

_____

_____

_____

_____

_____

_____

_____

_____

_____

_____

_____

_____

_____

_____

_____

_____

_____

Case Study Analysis

One of the many challenges within tourism is finding out its true economic impact, and, therefore, importance to a community, region, or country. London-based company Oxford Economics is one of the few rising to this challenge and helping destinations and companies quantify their tourism income.

So why is it so difficult to measure tourism and its impact? Compared to other industries, for example financial services, insurance or construction, tourism stands out as difficult to define. And to be able to measure something, one must define it. The major obstacle is that tourism runs across different industries, based on demand. For example, a restaurant is likely to have local customers as well as visitors. Other sectors tourism touches upon are lodging, recreation, retail, real estate, air passenger transport, food & beverage, car rentals, taxi services, and many others.

To overcome this challenge, the United Nation's World Tourism Organization (WTO) created the tourism satellite account (TSA). This defines the tourism industry and helps measure its impact on an economically comparable scale. The TSA is used throughout the world and has been confirmed by the UN, Eurostat and OECD (Organisation for Economic Co-operation and Development). The definition coined by WTO is as follows:

> **Tourism Industry**: *Measures the value of traveller activity within "tourism characteristic industries". This concept measures only the direct impact of the travel industry.*

However, there's a lot more to tourism's impact on the economy and the second definition provided by the WTO creates a way to measure the wider effect. Where the 'Tourism Industry' measures the direct impact of travel and tourism spend, the following definition also looks at the indirect and induced spend that travel infers.

> **Tourism Economic Impact**: *Includes the tourism industry plus government spending and capital investment in support of tourism. This is the basis of the total economic impact analysis, including direct, indirect and induced impacts.*

With the work done by WTO, there's now a framework and methodology in place to overcome the challenge and measure tourism in its own right, as well as on its extended scale. Let's take a look at how Oxford Economics helped one US state understand their tourism economy: in 2014, New Jersey employed 315,952 people in tourism – making it the 6th largest employer in the private sector. Furthermore, tourism sales resulted in state and local taxes collection to the amount of $4.6 billion. This means each household would have to be taxed an additional $1,460 per year if the tourism industry didn't exist anymore. You can clearly see why measuring this information is important to many stakeholders.

For more information on Oxford Economics and their work in New Jersey in particular, have a look online and find 'The Economic Impact of Tourism in New Jersey' report on the 'Visit New Jersey' website. Have a read through the material and then come back to answer the following questions:

(1) Explain in your own words what makes it so difficult to measure tourism. Then think about adding the complexities of business travel into the mix: how can you obtain correct information?

_____

_____

_____

_____

_____

_____

_____

_____

_____

_____

_____

_____

_____

_____

_____

_____

_____

_____

_____

_____

_____

(2) What is the TSA and why was it set-up in the first place?

_____

_____

_____

_____

_____

_____

_____

_____

_____

_____

_____

_____

_____

_____

_____

_____

_____

_____

_____

_____

(3) How important is tourism to the state of New Jersey – a state that's not particularly known for tourism? What about where you live? Does your town or county rely on tourism?

_____

_____

_____

_____

_____

_____

_____

_____

_____

_____

_____

_____

_____

_____

_____

_____

_____

_____

_____

Corporate Travel, Management & the Global Economy

Corporate travel is an important part of the big picture of tourism – not only business travel. While thinking of an individual traveller going abroad for business might not sound exciting or complicated, the sheer mass of individuals travelling for their (i.e. one) company shows a different picture.

Consider, for instance, that IBM in the US alone spent $590 million just on air transactions in 2013. And that total business-travel spend in the US was over $280 billion in 2014.

Critical Thinking

Consider what you already know about tourism overall. Think about how corporate travel differs, but also what similarities there are or might be.

(1) Define corporate travel in your own words:

_____

_____

_____

_____

_____

_____

_____

_____

_____

_____

_____

_____

_____

_____

_____

_____

(2) How does corporate travel differ from leisure tourism?

(3) In your opinion, is a corporate travel programme really necessary? Why?

_____

_____

_____

_____

_____

_____

_____

_____

_____

_____

_____

_____

_____

_____

_____

_____

_____

_____

_____

_____

Research

Now that you're a little clearer about corporate travel and its place within tourism, it's time to delve deeper into the topic.

Go online to Buying Business Travel, a corporate travel media site. Search for "duty of care" and "corporate travel programme". While reading the articles, think about your answer to the last question above.

If you want to stay up-to-date on developments in corporate travel, it might be an idea to sign up for the newsletter and / or the physical magazine.

Once you have a good understanding of duty of care for companies and in particular what this means for corporate travel, try to answer this question:

(1) How has your opinion of travel programmes changed? If it hasn't changed, how would you argue the case for or against a travel programme now?

_____

_____

_____

_____

_____

_____

_____

_____

_____

_____

_____

_____

_____

_____

Case Study Analysis

Another study conducted by Oxford Economics in 2009 gives insight into the relationship between corporate travel and company performance. Over a period of 13 years, data from 14 economic sectors was captured and analysed. Notice that the findings were published at the height of the economic crisis, and cutting costs was a major topic for most companies around the world.

The challenge for companies is to find a balance between spending exuberantly on travel and entertainment and skimping on travel costs. Naturally, both have an impact on the traveling employees, as well as on their work performance. When focusing on cost savings, travellers might have to take a red-eye flight (i.e. travel overnight) for an all-important meeting the next morning. Tying budgets too closely might also effect duty of care, as hotels might be chosen that are cheap but in unsafe neighbourhoods. On the flip side of that spectrum, spending too much can be seen as bribing, which is a criminal offence and can have very adverse effects on the individual, but also on the company.

Let's stick with the frugal end of the spectrum: cost cutting. When considering travel as an investment, it's clear that a reduction in that investment has an impact not only on the travellers themselves, but also on the company as a whole. It's not surprising that Oxford Economics found that companies who made significant cuts to their travel budgets found they were losing clients as well.

Not traveling, that is, not engaging with customers and suppliers face-to-face, sends a very strong message to the market: "we can't afford to travel". This in turn results in loss of trust with clients unsure about the state of health of the organization. It might not always result in loss of clients, but it would mostly put at least a damper on revenue and new sales opportunities.

Let's have a look at some staggering numbers from the Oxford Economics study:

- ➤ Every $1 = $12,50 in increased revenue, and $3,80 in profits

- ➤ About 28% of current business would be lost without face-to-face meetings

- ➤ About 40% of prospects are converted in person

- ➤ About 85% of executives felt virtual alternatives (like web meetings) weren't a viable option for new business discussions

- ➤ More than half of corporate travellers feel that internal company is key to professional development and job performance

(All figures in this book are quoted in US dollars.)

It's tempting to go with a simple solution: keep traveling and your revenues will grow, clients will trust you and stay with you and you'll be able to convert new sales opportunities. It helps build relationships, externally with clients and prospects, but also internally with colleagues and across departments. But as mentioned in the beginning of this case: there's a fine balance to strike to make sure travel budgets aren't exhausted for the wrong reasons.

(1) What's the biggest challenge companies face when cutting down on travel?

_____

_____

_____

_____

_____

_____

_____

_____

_____

_____

_____

_____

_____

_____

_____

_____

_____

_____

_____

_____

_____

_____

_____

_____

(2) Would you consider travel as an investment? Why / Why not?

_____

_____

_____

_____

_____

_____

_____

_____

_____

_____

_____

_____

_____

_____

_____

_____

_____

_____

_____

_____

_____

(3) What would you say to your boss / company if they wanted to cut travel spend?

_____

_____

_____

_____

_____

_____

_____

_____

_____

_____

_____

_____

_____

_____

_____

_____

_____

_____

_____

_____

_____

_____

MICE – Meetings, Incentives, Conferences & Events

Corporate travel is part of the larger playing field of business travel. The meetings industry, incentive trips, conferences, exhibitions and events all fall under this spectrum. They're often put together under the acronym 'MICE'.

Since a lot of corporate travel can be attributed in some form to these categories, it makes sense to look at this sector to have a better understanding of how it all fits together.

Critical Thinking

This discussion around the MICE industry is not going to be very detailed, but we focus instead on the synergies between it and corporate travel. The following questions and exercises reflect this.

(1) What do you associate with the MICE sector?

_____

_____

_____

_____

_____

_____

_____

_____

_____

_____

_____

_____

(2) What commonalities do you see between MICE and corporate travel?

_____

_____

_____

_____

_____

_____

_____

_____

_____

_____

_____

_____

_____

_____

_____

_____

_____

_____

_____

_____

(3) Why do you think MICE attracts more attention and support at universities than corporate travel?

_____

_____

_____

_____

_____

_____

_____

_____

_____

_____

_____

_____

_____

_____

_____

_____

_____

_____

_____

_____

Research

In corporate travel, the most important part of MICE is meetings. These have quite a lot of commonalities and therefore lend themselves to make the travel programme better.

For this research exercise, go to the Advito website and find out about the ITM programme. ITM stands for 'integrating travel and meetings', which already gives you an inkling about what you're looking for.

Once you've read through the website and material you find, have a go at answering this question:

(1) In your opinion, how worthwhile is it for a company to implement ITM to their travel programme? Give reasons for your answer.

_____

_____

_____

_____

_____

_____

_____

_____

_____

_____

_____

_____

_____

_____

_____

_____

Case Study Analysis

For the case study, we also stick with the topic of ITM. During the research assignment you might have already come across Advito's white paper on the topic. If not, it might be worthwhile downloading a copy to further your understanding of this initiative. Note that it's not only Advito who is offering ITM, but that the industry as a whole is moving towards integrating travel and meetings.

Travel and meetings have traditionally not been in the same department. Where travel looks after individual travellers and the annual contracts with suppliers, meetings looks after groups and sets up events in venues that often change. But with the economic crisis of 2008/2009, companies tightened their travel budgets (as you've read about in the preceding case study). This led to travel managers and other stakeholders looking again to see where savings could be made without compromising productivity and the safety of travellers.

Let's look at some numbers to make a case for meetings and events within corporate travel:

➤ More than 35% of the overall travel budget is spent on meetings and events

➤ About 80% of all meetings and events are organised outside of policy

Looking at these figures, there's clearly room for improvement and, more importantly, savings. The first step is to approach meetings and events just like corporate travel: from a strategic point of view. A Strategic Meetings Management Programme (SMMP) means organisers follow travel policy (although there might be some exceptions to the rule) and negotiate deals with suppliers. These deals are often with particular venues which are booked somewhat regularly throughout the year.

Implementing SMMP allows organisers and other stakeholders to manage meetings and event spend better, as data is more transparent and measured against key performance indicators (KPIs).

But this is only the first step, and to truly bring savings (and benefits) for the company, the SMMP needs to be integrated with corporate travel. This means consolidating spend and finding hotels and venues that work for both: individual travellers and groups. Once ITM is in place, the travel manager is in charge of negotiating supplier deals once again.

The integration also allows the travel manager to fine-tune travel policy to meetings and group needs (or issue a separate version for those). Whichever way they choose (and is best for the company), ITM sits within one place and is steered – which has a number of benefits:

➤ Better supplier relations (through better data, better compliance, and more spending power)

➤ Better risk management (knowing where travellers are – even when they're at events)

➤ Better employee satisfaction (everything is happening in one place; ease of use)

➤ Better spend and programme management (data is measured and actions can be taken)

➤ Better resources (as knowledge from travel and meetings is shared across the board)

With so many benefits it's hard to imagine ITM hasn't surfaced earlier. But have a look at the questions and come up with your own opinions on how worthwhile this strategy is.

(1) How would you go about strategically setting up a meetings department?

(2) Why are companies interested in ITM?

_____

_____

_____

_____

_____

_____

_____

_____

_____

_____

_____

_____

_____

_____

_____

_____

_____

_____

_____

_____

(3) What do you think are the drawbacks to consolidating travel and meetings?

Virtual Meetings

To round off this part about corporate travel within the wider tourism landscape, let's consider virtual meetings and, with that, virtual collaboration. When the virtual hype started, it was thought to have a dramatic impact on business travel. Advocates said that the need for meeting in person would be eliminated through technology and virtual 'face-to-face' options.

However, so far, it hasn't come to that. Although virtual collaboration is an everyday occurrence, they're supplementing travel rather than substituting it – at least for the moment.

Critical Thinking

Assuming that you use means of virtual collaboration (chat features, Skype, Facetime, etc.) in your private life, try to answer the following questions before doing the research exercise.

(1) How would you differentiate virtual meetings from virtual collaboration?

_____

_____

_____

_____

_____

_____

_____

_____

_____

_____

_____

_____

(2) What is your opinion on virtual meetings for business?

_____

_____

_____

_____

_____

_____

_____

_____

_____

_____

_____

_____

_____

_____

_____

_____

_____

_____

_____

_____

_____

(3) Do you think virtual meetings will make physical travel redundant? Why?

_____

_____

_____

_____

_____

_____

_____

_____

_____

_____

_____

_____

_____

_____

_____

_____

_____

_____

_____

_____

_____

_____

Research

Now that you've formed an opinion about virtual meetings and virtual collaboration, have a look online by doing a basic search on what results show when looking these words up. Consider whether they mention travel at all, that is, do companies try to position their solutions as substitutes for travel?

After searching and reading some of the information available, return here to answer the following question:

(1) Imagine you are part of a global and virtual team. What are your five key tips for collaborating effectively (and virtually)?

_____

_____

_____

_____

_____

_____

_____

_____

_____

_____

_____

_____

_____

_____

_____

_____

Case Study Analysis

Looking at corporate travel, we used a study by Oxford Economics released in 2009 regarding the necessity of travel – and not only the necessity, but also its value to the business's bottom line. In this part, however, we're now looking at the opposite: virtual collaboration.

Cisco is a company providing virtual collaboration experiences: from web-conferencing to actual tele-presence. The report referenced for this case was released in 2008 (you can find it by searching online for 'Cisco telepresence benefits case study'). Between 2006 and 2008 Cisco implemented 238 telepresence units across almost 130 locations worldwide. This was a huge investment and it wasn't clear at that time whether it would pay off in the long run.

Once implemented, the telepresence units were monitored closely, to find out about utilisation and user feedback. Their findings were encouraging (and contrary to Oxford Economics' research):

Facts	What this means for Cisco
238 telepresence units deployed globally	Utilisation rate on average 45% (target was 40%)
More than 105,000 meetings held between late 2006 and mid 2008 • Including about 13,000 customer meetings	More interaction with customers increased the sales closing rate. It also reduced the sales-cycle time.
Travel avoidance for about 17,500 meetings	Measured benefits are twofold: • About $90m cost avoidance estimate • Estimate of about 20m cubic meters of emissions eliminated
More than 4,800 multi-point meetings	Improved employee productivity is estimated at $40m

This table is an amended reproduction of the information in the original case study.

Cisco's data shows that 38% of meetings were internal ones, 31% were with customers and for 30% the reason was 'travel avoidance' – however, it is unclear from the report whether this would have been internal or external related travel.

However, 2008 is a long time ago, especially for technological advancements. Today, telepresence and other virtual collaboration tools aren't so expensive to implement – and they're getting much better and more reliable. In the industry, the feeling is generally that they won't replace travel – at least not in the near future – but with travel risks increasing, that might change more quickly than we think.

For the moment, it's felt that virtual collaboration is needed to keep the momentum going, to keep conversations across a distance throughout a project – and not to have to pinpoint everything at one face-to-face meeting.

(1) What's the biggest challenge using virtual communication rather than meet face-to-face?

---

(2) Why do you think Cisco succeeded, when Oxford Economics' study showed very different results about virtual collaboration?

_____

_____

_____

_____

_____

_____

_____

_____

_____

_____

_____

_____

_____

_____

_____

_____

_____

_____

_____

_____

_____

(3) If you were a travel manager, would you want to implement virtual collaboration? How would you distinguish between 'need-to-travel' and 'nice-to-travel'?

_____

_____

_____

_____

_____

_____

_____

_____

_____

_____

_____

_____

_____

_____

_____

_____

_____

_____

_____

Things to Remember

➤ One out of 11 jobs can be traced to tourism worldwide and the sector supports 9% of global GDP.

➤ In 2014, more than $3.2 billion was spent by just 10 companies for air bookings in the US alone.

➤ In the UK, 76 universities offer a total of 450 degrees in tourism – none of which offer corporate (or business) travel in the curriculum.

➤ Academics divide business travel into four categories:

  • Meetings
  • Conferences / Exhibitions / Events
  • Incentives
  • Individual business travel (i.e. corporate travel)

CORPORATE TRAVEL:
Past, Present, and Future

The real voyage of discovery consists not in seeking new landscapes but in having new eyes.

~ Marcel Proust

Checklist

By the end of this part you'll be able to:

✓ Explain the origins of corporate travel and how these relate to today's tourism industry.

✓ Know key dates, people and developments in the corporate travel industry.

✓ Develop an understanding of the current situation of the industry, including the challenges it's facing.

✓ Think about trends that might have an impact on corporate travel.

Introduction

3,500 years of history. That's what corporate travel can look back on. Early trading amongst communities reaches even further into history, but it was the Egyptians, under Pharaoh Hatshepsut, who made the first recorded trade trips across the sea. Yet today, we often tend to forget this history, as well as the reasons we travel.

The origins of corporate travel lie with those who travelled for trade, for knowledge, for innovation and for education. From the New Kingdom of Egypt across the Persian Empire and to the Roman Empire, culminating in travel across multiple kingdoms and realms from Europe to China on the Silk Road, it spans explorers like Marco Polo, Christopher Columbus and Thomas Cook as well as the World Expositions in Paris, London and New York.

The past 100 years have seen exponential growth of corporate travel: transportation has developed in leaps and bounds – so much so that one can take a business trip to Beijing, China, from London, and be back within 48 hours. The same 'business trip' Marco Polo made took about 10 years.

Finally, we move on to the current situation and future trends within corporate travel. What might be the next big thing? This section encourages you to think about what is currently out there – in terms of travel and beyond – and what you think will have the biggest impact in five or ten years.

The Past: 1500 BC to 1900 AD

There are several reasons to travel for business. In ancient history it started with trading, but soon developed to share and collect knowledge. The next stage was traveling for innovation, that is, taking something one has seen or experienced in one place, and transferring it to another situation. From thereon, travel for education and exploration developed, which still often incorporated parts of the aforementioned reasons to travel.

Traveling by foot, by boat, by cart or horse were the options for ancient travellers. Roads were perilous and it wasn't always certain that one would come back. But keep moving, they did.

Critical Thinking

The following three questions are all about history. If in doubt, have a read of the second chapter in the book, or go online and search for some of the explorers and find out about their journeys.

(1) What were the reasons to travel in ancient times?

In your own words, describe the main reasons discussed. What other reasons can you think of? Which one would be the most important for you?

_____

_____

_____

_____

_____

_____

_____

_____

_____

_____

_____

_____

(2) What would you have done?

Imagine you're living in ancient times (your choice of century and empire): what would you have done? What would have been your focus for traveling?

_____

_____

_____

_____

_____

_____

_____

_____

_____

_____

_____

_____

_____

_____

_____

_____

_____

_____

_____

_____

(3) How did travel over this time (1500 BC to 1900 AD) shape our world?

It's a big question, but try to think about the achievements, the trade and the knowledge shared.

_____

_____

_____

_____

_____

_____

_____

_____

_____

_____

_____

_____

_____

_____

_____

_____

_____

Research

The critical thinking questions have hopefully immersed you fully in the heritage of corporate travel. So you're well equipped for the research exercise.

Go online and find information about the East India Tea Company. Reading up on the history of this company, think about how trade and travel worked together to create this firm that's still operating today.

After reading, try to answer this question:

(1) Link the reasons for traveling, as discussed previously, to the trade of the East India Tea Company. What evidence can you find for the different reasons?

_____

_____

_____

_____

_____

_____

_____

_____

_____

_____

_____

_____

_____

_____

_____

Case Study Analysis

For our case study, let's look at the ancient trading network widely known as 'Silk Road'. This connected the Chinese city of Xi'an by road to Istanbul, Turkey. Records show that trade started as early as 500 BC.

Silk fabric can be traced back in Europe to around 500 BC, however, trading became more frequent under the Han Dynasty (202 BC-9 AD). Naturally, many more commodities were traded on this route, and the name was only been coined in the 19th century.

Traveling and trading about 2,000 years ago was a dangerous business, especially, if it involved going through foreign lands and on rough terrain. There were warring tribes to worry about, as well as the Taklimakan desert. And, although the map below doesn't show it, there was also a route through the Himalayan mountains too, that came with yet more challenges.

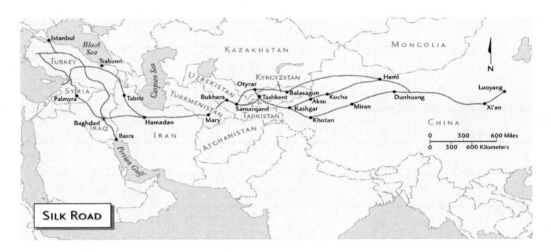

Silk Road: from Luoyang to Istanbul   *Credit: Eurasia Travel*

Finally, during the Tang Dynasty (618-906 AD) and under the rule of Emperor Taizong, the overland trade routes were made and kept safe: he secured peace with the nomadic tribes from the north and northwest. It was partly due to this peace that safe passage was ensured, and made the Silk Road an international network – famous even today.

Another activity that increased travel and trade was the tendency to only move goods along certain sections of the road. Merchants would buy or trade wares and bring them along a stretch of road they were familiar with. They'd then sell (or exchange) their goods and travel back, whilst the wares would slowly make their way west. Some items, naturally, didn't get very far this way as they were traded en route, thus driving prices upwards.

(1) What are the main challenges traveling and trading on the Silk Road?

_____

_____

_____

_____

_____

_____

_____

_____

_____

_____

_____

_____

_____

_____

_____

_____

_____

_____

_____

_____

_____

(2) How does the trading network shown on the map differ from today's trading routes? How is it similar?

_____

_____

_____

_____

_____

_____

_____

_____

_____

_____

_____

_____

_____

_____

_____

_____

_____

_____

_____

_____

_____

(3) How does trading differ today? Think about the phrase 'cutting out the middle man'.

_____

_____

_____

_____

_____

_____

_____

_____

_____

_____

_____

_____

_____

_____

_____

_____

_____

_____

_____

_____

_____

The Past: the Last 100 Years

The last 100 years has seen tremendous achievements, especially in transportation: the aircraft was invented and in the 1930s Boeing introduced the first flight attendant to its planes. But there have also been great achievements in technology, going hand-in-hand with transportation. Planes are bigger, can take more load and people, and can go further. Other technological developments bring us reservation systems, and jumping years ahead, are enabling us now to make travel decisions on our phones.

Critical Thinking

Knowing that you have experienced with travel yourself, try to think back some years and remember (or imagine) what it was like when we weren't tied to our phones and tablets.

(1) What for you is the most significant development of the last 100 years?

_____

_____

_____

_____

_____

_____

_____

_____

_____

_____

_____

_____

_____

(2) Compared to ancient history, what development surprises you most?

_____

_____

_____

_____

_____

_____

_____

_____

_____

_____

_____

_____

_____

_____

_____

_____

_____

_____

_____

_____

(3) And what do you consider might have been more developed by now?

_____

_____

_____

_____

_____

_____

_____

_____

_____

_____

_____

_____

_____

_____

_____

_____

_____

_____

_____

_____

_____

_____

Research

For research into the past 100 years, please have a look at the 9/11 attacks in the US. These aren't necessarily related to the subject of this book, but they are an important (and sad) milestone for corporate travel. Research information about what happened, and more specifically, what happened to travel afterwards.

When you're done, please answer the following question:

(1) What impact did the 9/11 attacks have on corporate travel in particular?

_____

_____

_____

_____

_____

_____

_____

_____

_____

_____

_____

_____

_____

_____

_____

_____

_____

_____

Case Study Analysis

One of the big changes over the last 100 years is, of course, air travel; and the somewhat matter-of-fact attitude we have towards it today. But back in the 1950s it was a big deal to travel by air, not only for the passengers, but also for the people working for the airlines. Reservations and ticketing was a manual and time-consuming process.

Let's focus on American Airlines whose reservation and ticketing at that time averaged 90 minutes per booking. It involved up to eight reservation agents in their headquarters, looking at physical charts of aircrafts and marking these to keep track with what was booked and available. It also involved travel agents who'd phone in to enquire about a connection. They sometimes had to wait up to three hours before a reservation could be confirmed (or declined).

This process was inefficient, time consuming and costly, and it couldn't cope with the growth air travel was embarking on.

It was with a bit of luck then, that IBM's Blair Smith, a senior sales figure, and American Airlines' president C. R. Smith found themselves sitting next to each other on a flight from Los Angeles to New York. They got talking, and Blair Smith discussed the recent SAGE project with C. R. This was a computer-based messaging system using teleprinters for information input as well as output.

The two men quickly came to the conclusion that this might be the idea American Airlines was waiting for, and in 1957 a formal research agreement was signed by the two companies to work together on the *Semi-Automated Business Research Environment* – which was to become SABRE.

While this might sound like a perfect solution, it wasn't an instant hit. As always is the case, there's a lot of uncertainty and angst about change – especially when the change is as big as bringing teleprinters to over 100 locations across the US. The reservation system struggled with external adoption, that is travel agents making use of the new technology, as well as internal adoption.

Adoption became more widespread in the 1970s and by the 1980s American Airlines found, through research, that travel agents generally booked the first item on the flight search result list. Further research confirmed this and led to American Airlines showing their own flights ahead of the competition; after all it was their own reservation system. However, the United States government outlawed screen bias in 1984.

Today, Sabre is a company in its own right, and one of several global distribution systems (GDS) servicing the travel industry.

(1) When you buy an airline ticket, how long does it usually take you to select an option and receive the airline's confirmation of booking?

_____

_____

_____

_____

_____

_____

_____

_____

_____

_____

_____

_____

_____

_____

_____

_____

_____

_____

_____

(2) Time and efficiencies go hand-in-hand with technology: what could American Airlines have done to get better adoption rates early on?

_____

_____

_____

_____

_____

_____

_____

_____

_____

_____

_____

_____

_____

_____

_____

_____

_____

_____

_____

(3) How do you feel about the use of screen bias?

Present: Where Are We Now?

While there are many changes and advances in corporate travel, particularly in technology and mobile options, the reasons to travel remain unchanged: trading, sharing knowledge and education, innovation and exploring.

Today's corporate travel industry is focussed on the travel programme: negotiations, savings, duty of care, travel risk management, payments and expenses, but also traveller engagement.

Critical Thinking

Corporate travel has a lot of complexities that aren't immediately visible when looking at the business traveller. The travel programme guidance, the travel policy to follow, the duty of care considerations, personal and data safety, payment options and reimbursements are among some of the things happening in the background.

(1) What do you think is the biggest change from past to present?

_____

_____

_____

_____

_____

_____

_____

_____

_____

_____

_____

_____

_____

(2) What, in your opinion, is the biggest challenge for corporate travel today?

_____

_____

_____

_____

_____

_____

_____

_____

_____

_____

_____

_____

_____

_____

_____

_____

_____

_____

_____

_____

(3) How do Travel Management Companies (TMCs) fit into corporate travel?

_____

_____

_____

_____

_____

_____

_____

_____

_____

_____

_____

_____

_____

_____

_____

_____

_____

_____

_____

_____

Research

One of the recurring topics in corporate travel is travel risk management. You'll have found out about the changes to the industry after 9/11 in the last research exercise. Today, we're facing new challenges and more terror attacks than ever before.

Find out what people are talking about in corporate travel: how is the view towards travel risk management changing? What measures are they putting in place? When you're done, answer the following question:

(1) What are the big trends currently for travel risk management in corporate travel?

_____

_____

_____

_____

_____

_____

_____

_____

_____

_____

_____

_____

_____

_____

_____

Case Study Analysis

One of the current topics in corporate travel is behaviour management. Actually, it's a topic that recurs time and again as new technological advances offer fresh options to entice travellers to behave a certain way. In essence, behaviour management is about influencing the decision of which supplier to use (or what product to buy) when travelling.

The reason behaviour management is almost constantly at the forefront of travel managers' minds is that travellers are often not booking within travel policy. Hence the company can't fulfil their duty of care obligations or help in an emergency, simply because they don't know where the traveller is. Compliance goes hand in hand with behaviour and once more technology is here to save the day.

One of the hype topics discussed in regards to behaviour management is 'gamification'. Currently, travel managers employ this as one approach to engage with individual travellers or smaller groups (like departments). They have dashboards of top traveller in policy, or most miles and least spent, or some such, to showcase to employees what is actually possible and, naturally, makes others want to win, thereby upping compliance levels.

Another way to tempt travel policy compliance is the use of behavioural economics. As Dan Ariely's book, Predictably Irrational (2009) promises, travellers – just like everyone else – need to be nudged to make logical choices. This can be done by anchoring prices of different travel services so employees develop an understanding of what is a reasonable price for a certain product.

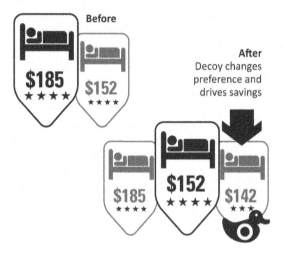

Decoy Pricing

The travel manager could also use framing for travel options, giving the traveller the feeling they choose 'the right thing' without knowing that their behaviour was actually steered. Another option is decoy pricing, which has a similar affect to framing as it puts the price in perspective.

Looking back at the Sabre case study in the preceding part, remember how American Airlines used screen bias to influence travel agents' choice of flight? In a way, behavioural economics does just that – but with employees traveling for business, who is to argue that this is unethical?

The possibilities of influencing travellers and reminding them of preferred behaviour are increasing by the day, once again thanks to technology, a deeper understanding of communications and the need for personalisation.

(1) What is gamification? How would you use it if you were a travel manager?

_____

_____

_____

_____

_____

_____

_____

_____

_____

_____

_____

_____

_____

_____

_____

_____

_____

_____

_____

_____

_____

(2) Describe the use of behavioural economics within corporate travel.

_____

_____

_____

_____

_____

_____

_____

_____

_____

_____

_____

_____

_____

_____

_____

_____

_____

_____

_____

_____

_____

_____

_____

(3) Do you think using screen bias within the corporate environment should be allowed? Why?

_____

_____

_____

_____

_____

_____

_____

_____

_____

_____

_____

_____

_____

_____

_____

_____

_____

_____

_____

_____

_____

Future: Gazing Into the Crystal Ball

Now let us look to the future. There are two differentiations I'd like to make: trends that are already being discussed currently in the media, and those that are starting to come up in other industries but might not yet have found a connection to corporate travel.

With the trends already in the public eye, note that it takes about two years for trends to make it into travel programmes – often longer. Going 'mainstream' might not happen for five years, that is, after trends have been tested by the more adventurous companies and proved worthwhile.

Critical Thinking

Trending topics are recurring from time to time, often when breakthrough advances have been made. Currently, hot topics in the industry are the sharing economy, hotel mergers and acquisitions, commission payments, and traveller engagement.

(1) Why do you think it takes so long for trends to become reality?

_____

_____

_____

_____

_____

_____

_____

_____

_____

_____

_____

_____

_____

(2) What trends are currently discussed in the media that you're most looking forward to?

_____

_____

_____

_____

_____

_____

_____

_____

_____

_____

_____

_____

_____

_____

_____

_____

_____

_____

_____

_____

(3) What corporate travel trends in other industries do you see that could affect the industry? How?

_____

_____

_____

_____

_____

_____

_____

_____

_____

_____

_____

_____

_____

_____

_____

_____

_____

_____

_____

_____

_____

_____

Research

Let's now have a look at one of the topics currently discussed: the sharing economy, or, as it is also known, the on-demand economy. They are the Airbnbs and Ubers – and their various smaller competitors, who are often found in local markets.

(1) How are these suppliers challenging the corporate travel market place?

_____

_____

_____

_____

_____

_____

_____

_____

_____

_____

_____

_____

_____

_____

_____

_____

Case Study Analysis

There are many trends out there that will have an impact on corporate travel and it's quite difficult to select just one for a case study. However, with some of the topics already discussed in this part, especially around duty-of-care and safety, self-driving cars seems to be a somewhat logical choice.

Many cars today already have some autonomous features installed: parking sensors, distance sensors during traffic and cruise control to name but a few. Yet the fully-autonomous driverless car is still some years away. And there are challenges that will need to be overcome before they become mainstream: for example, questions of insurance and safety regulations will need to be addressed.

For corporate travel, they're a useful option of the future: many travellers are fatigued after a (long-haul) flight and don't want to have to find a route to the hotel or office. Hence they opt for the more expensive option of a taxi or chauffeur-driven car – which is probably for the best as fatigued drivers pose a risk to overall traffic, and not only themselves.

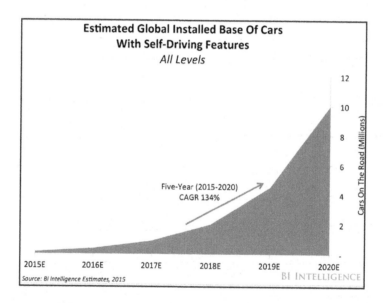

The graphic on the left shows BI Intelligence's research findings on how quickly cars with self-driving features will gain traction in the world; though the report acknowledges that actual driverless cars are a much longer way off.

Going back to the use of these cars in corporate travel, though, it's fair to say that car rental companies are often at the forefront of technology with new cars. It's a fact that part of their business (quite a large part at that) is the selling of one-year-old cars into the wider market place to make space for new models.

For travellers, having the peace of mind of just jumping into a (pre-booked) chauffeur-driven car is comforting. Having to go to the rental car desk, fill out forms and then find the car in the garage all adds to travel stress. Maybe once the self-driving cars line up conveniently at the airports and train stations and the traveller 'tells' it where to go by connecting the smart phone calendar this will actually take off in a big way?

(1) Would you want to be driven by a driverless car?

_____

_____

_____

_____

_____

_____

_____

_____

_____

_____

_____

_____

_____

_____

_____

_____

_____

_____

_____

_____

_____

(2) Do you believe driverless cars will be safer than when we drive ourselves? Why?

_____

_____

_____

_____

_____

_____

_____

_____

_____

_____

_____

_____

_____

_____

_____

_____

_____

_____

_____

_____

_____

_____

(3) If you were a travel manager, would you opt for self-driving cars (i.e. driverless) or chauffeur-driven cars? Give reasons for your answer.

_____

_____

_____

_____

_____

_____

_____

_____

_____

_____

_____

_____

_____

_____

_____

_____

_____

_____

_____

_____

Things to Remember

➤ International trade can be traced back to Egypt – roughly 3,500 years ago.

➤ Today, corporate travel is characterised by its complexities around schedules and choices.

➤ Trending topics of the year 2016 are the sharing economy, traveller engagement, personalisation, distribution channels, virtual payments, virtual collaboration and predictive and prescriptive analytics.

➤ Fast-forward to 2020 and this will become even more data- and technology-driven with the IoT (Internet of Things) and smart everythings (glasses, cars, cities – you name it).

Who is Who in Corporate Travel

*The great difference between voyages rests not with the ships,
but with the people you meet on them.*

~ Amelia E. Barr

Checklist

By the end of this part you'll be able to:

✓ Know who the key stakeholders are, what they do and how they add value to the industry.

✓ Have insights into other stakeholders that may be passively involved or have an impact on education.

✓ Develop an understanding of the many different roles and responsibilities in the corporate travel industry.

Introduction

This part introduces the stakeholders in corporate travel: the travel manager, travel management companies (TMCs), travel suppliers (such as airlines and hotels) and others that play a role today (consultants, the global distribution system (GDS) providers, associations as bodies of knowledge for the industry – and the travellers themselves).

The travel manager is an important figure, not only for the company who relies on their expertise of running a successful travel programme, but also for the many suppliers who want to be chosen as preferred partners and associations who want to exchange knowledge and education.

The TMCs also play an important role advising the travel managers and supporting global travel programmes. On the flip side, they also work closely with suppliers, offering feedback and guidance for becoming 'preferred' by a certain client. And let's not forget that it's the TMCs that actually facilitate the bookings and ticketing for their clients.

Yet, a travel programme can't be successful without the suppliers, those who provide the actual service to the traveller. Suppliers might be airlines, hotels or car rental companies. These are often called the big three. Rail is important in certain markets, like Europe, but not so important in others, like the US. And to make everything work seamlessly, other stakeholders are needed: the GDSs, consultants, associations, and many other technology firms that play a part in the big and complex machinery of corporate travel.

The Travel Manager

The travel manager has many hats to wear, as they're dealing with many different tasks. They have to be salespeople to 'sell' the travel programme internally to the employees of the company. They have to be procurers to negotiate the best deals with suppliers. They also have to be marketers to win support and buy-in from important stakeholders within the company. They have to be police officers, security managers, concierges, money-savers, news broadcasters and the list goes on.

Critical Thinking

Imagine yourself in the role of travel manager. It's your first week on the job and the hotel-negotiating season is about to start in earnest.

(1) What do you think would be the best part about being a travel manager?

_____

_____

_____

_____

_____

_____

_____

_____

_____

_____

_____

_____

_____

(2) And on the flip side, what would be the worst?

_____

_____

_____

_____

_____

_____

_____

_____

_____

_____

_____

_____

_____

_____

_____

_____

_____

_____

_____

_____

_____

_____

(3) What could you bring to the travel programme with the current skills you have?

_____

_____

_____

_____

_____

_____

_____

_____

_____

_____

_____

_____

_____

_____

_____

_____

_____

_____

_____

_____

_____

Research

Now you're more familiar with the role of the travel manager and your own likes and dislikes about the position, have a look online at an actual job advertisement for a corporate travel manager. Note that it's important to specify corporate/business travel manager in your search so you don't end up with leisure offers.

For example, at point of writing, a job search on reed.co.uk displayed over 800 results. Pick the first one, or one that sounds appealing to you and have a read of the description, the responsibilities and the skill-set the company is looking for. Then complete the following task:

(1) Make a list of all the responsibilities and skills of the job advert that you hadn't considered before as being important for a travel manager. Give reasons and think about why they might be important in this role.

_____

_____

_____

_____

_____

_____

_____

_____

_____

_____

_____

_____

_____

_____

_____

_____

Case Study Analysis

For this case study, let's look at one of the tasks a travel manager might come across: implementing a travel risk management (TRM) programme. As with everything the travel manager wants to put in place, it needs collaboration from many other internal and external stakeholders.

First, it's important the travel manager organises the information available from past trips and experiences of incidents. Data should always be at the beginning of every project that involves others, because it's easier to convince people of needs when information is clearly presented and proven.

Then it's time to get people involved. At this stage, the travel manager would talk to internal stakeholders only, like Human Resources, Information Technology, Security, Legal and the senior management team. It's necessary to have one project manager (this could be the travel manager themselves) and a project sponsor (someone high up in the 'food chain' who supports the initiative).

Likelihood		Impact		
Very likely	Medium 2	High 3	Extreme 5
Likely	Low 1	Medium 2	High 3
Unlikely	Low 1	Low 1	Medium 2
What is the chance it will happen?	Minor	Moderate	Major

Risk-mapping

With the team and the data in place, it's time to analyse the information and map future risks. A standard way of doing this looks something like the graphic to the right.

Note that going through past incidents and mapping risks isn't about scare-mongering, but rather about being prepared should something happen when employees are on the road. Too often, people don't think something will happen to them – and if it does, they're ill prepared and don't know what to do or who to turn to.

Once the risk mapping is done, the project team creates a risk matrix thereby defining the risks further, and where travellers might encounter them. At this stage it's advisable to bring in external stakeholders to the table: the TMC has a lot of experience with travel risk and can help with minor incidents. In most cases, however, it's advisable to bring in a specialist company as well.

When the theory and planning are done, it's time to put the plan into action – and that means communicating it to the travellers. They are the ones who should benefit from the information gathered, and the actions put in place to help them in need. But it can be tricky to reach them when they're on the road: often the contact details they supply are outdated (for example, when personal data changes but isn't updated on company records; or when an assistant books the trip and inputs their own details rather than the travellers').

That's why the last stage of the implementation should always be gathering feedback: finding out what works and what doesn't, and educating employees about TRM and where they can get help when they need it.

(1) Who are the key stakeholders for implementing a TRM programme?

_____

_____

_____

_____

_____

_____

_____

_____

_____

_____

_____

_____

_____

_____

(2) What is the main challenge for the travel manager? Why?

_____

_____

_____

_____

_____

_____

_____

_____

_____

_____

_____

_____

_____

_____

_____

_____

_____

_____

_____

_____

_____

(3) How can the travel manager ensure that travellers are aware of the TRM programme?

_____

_____

_____

_____

_____

_____

_____

_____

_____

_____

_____

_____

_____

_____

_____

_____

_____

_____

_____

_____

The Travel Management Company (TMC)

The TMC found its purpose in helping corporations with travel by booking, ticketing and servicing their travel requests. TMCs are different from traditional leisure travel agencies, because they don't only help with arrangements, but provide a full spectrum of services as well. These include planning and 'on-the-go' services, intelligence and analytics, travel risk management, demand and behaviour management, payment and expense management, as well as programme support and optimisation.

Critical Thinking

As the list of service categories above shows, the TMCs are dealing with a complex world and have to be expert in many subjects to be able to serve their clients.

(1) Explain the differences between leisure travel agencies and TMCs

_____

_____

_____

_____

_____

_____

_____

_____

_____

_____

_____

_____

_____

(2) How do you see the TMCs adding value to their customers?

_____

_____

_____

_____

_____

_____

_____

_____

_____

_____

_____

_____

_____

_____

_____

_____

_____

_____

_____

_____

_____

_____

_____

(3) Looking at planning and 'on-the-go' services, what do you think is offered?

_____

_____

_____

_____

_____

_____

_____

_____

_____

_____

_____

_____

_____

_____

_____

_____

_____

_____

_____

_____

_____

Research

As you might know (or have gathered from the little introduction) the bulk work of the TMC is still booking, ticketing and servicing travel requests. And that also means that the biggest part of the workforce in a TMC is the agents. However, you also know that technology is fast evolving and most people now book their trips online.

With that in mind, have a look at what TMCs are doing to prepare for the time 'post-agent', or, indeed, whether such a time is likely to come. Then head back here to answer the following question:

(1) How will TMCs have to change to meet future demands?

_____

_____

_____

_____

_____

_____

_____

_____

_____

_____

_____

_____

_____

_____

_____

_____

Case Study Analysis

Distribution is becoming more fragmented thanks to the internet. Suppliers take advantage of being able to directly access their clients – and now TMCs are trying to do the same.

In the past, corporate travel was very much the domain of B2B (business to business): the supplier (whether one of the big three or the TMCs) would talk to the travel manager and the company they represent directly. They would negotiate deals and service those for the travellers. And that is still happening, of course, and forms a large part of the corporate travel industry.

But when the first notions of NDC (new distribution capabilities) – an initiative spearheaded by IATA – came to the market place, suppliers began to see the increased value in marketing directly to those people actually consuming their services. Let's not forget that loyalty programmes have a long-standing history with airlines and hotel chains alike.

The TMCs are a unique case in this scenario: they provide the booking for travellers, but they don't actually fulfil it. It's always 'on behalf of'; for example, a traveller needs to go from London to New York. She rings the TMC and finds out multiple options. She selects one and travels. The suppliers she's chosen (airline and hotel) are the ones actually fulfilling the service. Yet that doesn't stop TMCs wanting to break into the B2C (business to consumer) market.

Enter mobile apps: most of the global TMCs today offer a mobile app. This serves the traveller with a one-stop-shop solution for their itinerary, so they have all the data in one place. Naturally, apps today can do much more than store information, and so TMCs are looking into monetising the offering. Converting the app to an online booking tool means travellers can now use it to book accommodation or flights on the go. Note that, to increase traction, usability and experience, the apps often have map services enabled so it's easy for travellers to find their way to the locations they need to get to.

What do travel managers make of these changes? It depends (as it always does) on the company and the company's culture. Some travel managers are very happy to support the roll-out of the preferred TMC app, because they see it as a way to service their travellers better. When there's no preferred app suggested by travel managers, most employees just use what they'd use when they travel for leisure. And that means lost data, lost negotiation power, and lost duty-of-care opportunity.

It goes without saying that companies are able to purchase 'white-label' solutions. That means they can customise apps to a certain extent (load their company logo and fonts; preload negotiated deals). This is often an added bonus as developing a complex mobile app is still rather costly.

(1) Do you think it's ok for suppliers to go directly to the consumer, i.e. corporate travellers? Why?

_____

_____

_____

_____

_____

_____

_____

_____

_____

_____

_____

_____

_____

_____

_____

_____

_____

_____

_____

_____

(2) Part of the TMCs armoury is mobile apps: do you think this is the right approach? Why?

_____

_____

_____

_____

_____

_____

_____

_____

_____

_____

_____

_____

_____

_____

_____

_____

_____

_____

_____

_____

(3) What is your advice to TMCs wanting to target corporate travellers directly?

_____

_____

_____

_____

_____

_____

_____

_____

_____

_____

_____

_____

_____

_____

_____

_____

_____

_____

_____

_____

_____

_____

The Travel Suppliers

Traditionally, corporate travel looks at three core suppliers: airlines, hotels and car rental. In Europe and some Asian countries, rail also plays an important part. For these big spend areas, air transactions are leading the way with about 45% of all travel spend. Hotel accounts for about 20%, car rental for about 5% and rail for about 4% (where applicable).

This still leaves about 30% unaccounted for: dining and entertainment, other ground transportation (like taxis) and mobile charges fall into this category. These are less easy to manage or negotiate contracts for, but new products, like Uber or Dinova, are paving the way to smarter options.

Critical Thinking

Suppliers are of critical importance in the corporate travel world. Previously, you've already looked at the bridge between the travel manager and the service providers: the TMC.

(1) What are the reasons for the percentage spend of the big three supply categories?

_____

_____

_____

_____

_____

_____

_____

_____

_____

_____

_____

_____

(2) How do these figures compare with your own thoughts about corporate travel spend?

_____

_____

_____

_____

_____

_____

_____

_____

_____

_____

_____

_____

_____

_____

_____

_____

_____

_____

_____

(3) How would you manage 'hidden spend' areas, like ground transportation, dining, entertainment and mobile costs?

_____

_____

_____

_____

_____

_____

_____

_____

_____

_____

_____

_____

_____

_____

_____

_____

_____

_____

_____

_____

Research

You may already have seen in the news that the supplier Starwood Hotels is up for sale, and Marriott have put in an offer which is likely to be accepted (at time of writing). This merger would create the biggest global hotel supplier. But there's a lot to do before it happens.

Have a look at information about the merger and the difficulties. You might also want to read up about other bidders trying to woo Starwood.

(1) What will the biggest challenges be for a corporate travel management programme when the merger goes ahead?

_____

_____

_____

_____

_____

_____

_____

_____

_____

_____

_____

_____

_____

_____

_____

Case Study Analysis

The research exercise you've just completed has given you insights into the world of accommodation. For the case study, let's look at airlines. Low cost carriers (LCCs) for some time now have been breaking into the corporate travel market.

For a long time, LCCs didn't consider global distribution systems (GDSs) as a viable (read 'profitable') distribution channel. But in 2014, even Ryanair boss Michael O'Leary admitted this to be wrong. Corporate travellers are just too lucrative a segment not to target. And travel managers want to purchase via comparable channels, that is GDS.

The problem for travel managers is rogue bookings: bookings made outside the company booking tool. This is (sadly) common practice for hotel stays, but traditionally air transactions are mostly done through the right channels. Yet when LCCs started offering more and more scheduled flights to and from destinations easily accessible to corporate travellers, travel managers feared employees might jump on the bandwagon.

Travel managers were confirmed of this fear with posts appearing about new booking capabilities called 'open booking' – meaning travellers could book any way they wish and data would be uploaded automatically into the corporate channels. It sounds too good to be true. And it isn't. Travellers still have to forward itineraries to different email addresses and hope all data is loaded; the duty of care implications are severe; and at the moment there's not too much uptake on the traveller side, but with technological advances especially mobile, it's only a matter of time before ease of use and safety are married-up successfully.

In the interim, LCCs opt to cooperate with the GDSs: like easyJet with Amadeus (there is a case study available if you want to read up on this further). So why were (or are) LCCs reluctant to distribute their services through the GDS? Because they cost money to use. Airlines have to pay the GDS in order to be listed on this distribution channel. And while development is underway to make distribution easier and allow apple-to-apple comparison across different platforms, this hasn't advanced as much as the industry would like. To read up on the developments, check out NDC and IATA.

For travel managers, this slow development is good news: they have more time to prepare for NDC and had more leverage to bring LCCs onto the GDS table. And this makes it now possible for travel managers to assess LCC offers and compare them to the other airlines they're working with. At the same time, travellers can book LCC services through corporate channels.

(1) As a corporate traveller, would you want to fly LCCs? Explain your answer.

_____

_____

_____

_____

_____

_____

_____

_____

_____

_____

_____

_____

_____

_____

_____

_____

_____

_____

_____

_____

(2) As a travel manager, would you negotiate with LCCs and integrate them into your programme?

_____

_____

_____

_____

_____

_____

_____

_____

_____

_____

_____

_____

_____

_____

_____

_____

_____

_____

(3) What do you think is going to happen in the airline industry within the next five to ten years? Will there be more or less LCCs? Hybrid options?

_____

_____

_____

_____

_____

_____

_____

_____

_____

_____

_____

_____

_____

_____

_____

_____

_____

_____

_____

Other Travel Stakeholders

Alongside travel managers, TMCs and the 'big three' (or four), there are a number of other corporate travel stakeholders worth looking at. These are technology providers, like the global distribution systems (GDSs) discussed in the previous case study; consultants who act for travel managers and companies to create the best possible travel programme and often help with communications as well; associations who educate and inform the industry at large; and finally the travellers themselves.

The following exercises and questions are geared towards furthering your understanding of who else plays a part in the fragmented world of corporate travel.

Critical Thinking

The brief introduction gives you an overview of other players in corporate travel, but not an exhaustive list. Indeed, that would be difficult to come by. Have a think and try to build your own.

(1) What other stakeholders can you think of?

_____

_____

_____

_____

_____

_____

_____

_____

_____

_____

_____

(2) What is their role in corporate travel?

_____

_____

_____

_____

_____

_____

_____

_____

_____

_____

_____

_____

_____

_____

_____

_____

_____

_____

_____

_____

_____

(3) And which of these do you consider the most important? Explain your thinking.

_____

_____

_____

_____

_____

_____

_____

_____

_____

_____

_____

_____

_____

_____

_____

_____

_____

_____

_____

_____

Research

Let's look more closely at the associations helping the industry. The global ones are well known: GBTA (Global Business Travel Association) and ACTE (Association of corporate Travel Executives). Both offer a range of in-person as well as virtual events for their members. They have local and regional chapters to cater for localised issues. There are also several smaller associations truly focussing only on local groups. These sometimes partner with the global associations for events.

Have a look at websites of the associations. Definitely check the global ones, but maybe also try to find a local organisation to see the differences in their service offering. Then return to the following question.

(1) Why are associations so important for the corporate travel industry?

_____

_____

_____

_____

_____

_____

_____

_____

_____

_____

_____

_____

_____

_____

_____

_____

Case Study Analysis

Restaurants might have made your list. They provide dining and entertainment to travellers on the road, yet they're not part of negotiated deals. That's why the industry often speaks of 'hidden costs'. The travel manager only comes to know of these costs when the expense reports are updated.

Part of the travel manager's job is to keep an eye on costs and to budget for the year. Therefore, costs for dining and entertainment need to be known or estimated. This means that waiting for expense reports to understand on-trip spending and behaviour isn't the best solution. In case you're unfamiliar with the process: employees claim expenses once they're back from a trip. Some companies have a set time limit during which to claim expenses (for instance up to four weeks after travel). However, often it's left to the employee to take the time and do the paperwork.

Total cost of trip is often considered the Holy Grail in corporate travel management, because it's so difficult to piece together all the costs for just one trip. It sounds easy enough because we think the information is readily available, but more often than not it isn't. For example, a true picture of trip cost can only be painted with the booking information, invoice and consumption during the trip. That data is captured in various systems: online booking tool or call centre agent, supplier of services received (like airline or hotel) and receipts for on-the-go expenses like dining and entertainment costs. These data streams are consolidated and often enriched with corporate credit card data – but it does take time. Reports are often only ready about six weeks after a month ends (e.g. a report for January would be ready by mid-March) at least with all the information the company has access to at the time. It might be even longer when expense reports aren't created in a timely fashion.

Because of the delay in reporting and uncertainties around budgets for dining and entertainment, there are now companies helping travel managers create special programmes for their travellers. Dinova is one company offering to negotiate discounts for corporations at restaurant chains. This allows the travel manager access to more detailed and timely information, and the impact on the traveller is low: he just has to pay with the corporate credit card to receive the negotiated discount.

Naturally, managing yet another programme isn't without its own challenges:

> ➤ Communicating these new options to travellers

> ➤ Ensuring that the restaurants in the programme are the ones liked by the employees

> ➤ Enlisting enough restaurants in all destinations so people start using them

> ➤ Justifying the resources and costs to run the programme with the savings gained from it

For big corporations that have mature corporate travel programmes, this is a great opportunity to look at new options to save. For others it might be some time before exploring this area of hidden spend.

(1) Why do dining and entertainment costs present a challenge for travel managers?

_____

_____

_____

_____

_____

_____

_____

_____

_____

_____

_____

_____

_____

_____

_____

_____

_____

_____

_____

_____

_____

(2) As a traveller, would you opt for a restaurant suggested by your company?

_____

_____

_____

_____

_____

_____

_____

_____

_____

_____

_____

_____

_____

_____

_____

_____

_____

_____

(3) As a travel manager, would you be interested in integrating dining and entertainment into your travel programme?

_____

_____

_____

_____

_____

_____

_____

_____

_____

_____

_____

_____

_____

_____

_____

_____

_____

_____

_____

Things to Remember

➤ Corporate travel managers have many roles to play in their day-to-day lives; from communication expert to negotiation wizard, everything is possible – and needed.

➤ Travel Management Companies (TMCs) are a cornerstone of the corporate travel industry, providing advice and actions to travel managers – including booking travel arrangements.

➤ The big three travel suppliers are airlines, hotels and car rental companies. But there are many other players in this space.

➤ Not everyone is in it for their own sake; associations provide valuable insights to competitors, aiming to share information and educate the industry.

The Travel Programme

Remember what Bilbo used to say:
It's a dangerous business, Frodo, going out your door. You step
onto the road, and if you don't keep your feet, there's no knowing
where you might be swept off to.

~ JRR Tolkien

> **Checklist**
>
> By the end of this part you'll be able to:
>
> ✓ Understand the basics of a managed travel programme.
>
> ✓ Recognise sourcing within corporate travel and decide when to use it.
>
> ✓ Develop an understanding of the operations, both big-picture and in detail, that the travel manager deals with on a daily (and annual) basis.

Introduction

Until now you've been thinking a lot about the basics of corporate travel: its importance to the economy, its historical and current development and its many and various stakeholders. Now it's time to look more closely at the travel programme. First up is travel policy: the benefits of policy and how to increase traveller (or rather employee) buy-in and ownership.

Up next is a more detailed look at sourcing. You now know the stakeholders, and this section raises questions about the actions of travel managers and procurement. You'll look at questions about the importance of sourcing and negotiations, as well as the practicalities of the RFPs (request for proposals). Don't forget that there are big differences in air and hotel sourcing.

But sourcing and travel policy aren't the only things travel managers have to deal with. There are tasks that recur annually, and those they're dealing with on a daily basis. Everything from bookings, travel disruptions, communications, demand and behaviour management, technology, payments and corporate social responsibility (CSR) is somewhere on a travel manager's to-do list. It's the basis for a successful travel programme and the backbone for the traveller to have a seamless experience.

Travel Policy

Travel policy sets guidelines and helps manage travel costs. Several studies suggest that travel spend is the second largest controllable spend within companies after salaries! And by implementing travel policy, companies could save between 10-15% of travel spend – provided their travellers are compliant, of course.

Depending on the company and its culture, travel policy could be one page long or cover 100 pages. It's everything the traveller may (or may not) do while planning, booking and travelling.

Critical Thinking

The importance of a travel policy is obvious. Or isn't it? In today's world a multi-page document might not be the best way to communicate with employees on the road. Use the following questions to make up your own mind.

(1) What is travel policy? And how is it used today?

_____

_____

_____

_____

_____

_____

_____

_____

_____

_____

_____

_____

_____

(2) How could a company link its overall goals to the travel programme?

_____

_____

_____

_____

_____

_____

_____

_____

_____

_____

_____

_____

_____

_____

_____

_____

_____

_____

_____

_____

_____

(3) Does a travel policy still have a place in an increasingly digital world?

_____

_____

_____

_____

_____

_____

_____

_____

_____

_____

_____

_____

_____

_____

_____

_____

_____

_____

_____

_____

Research

For this research exercise, go online and search for 'corporate travel policy'. What comes up? Mostly university travel policies, which are publicly available. Often companies won't publish their full travel policy online for all to see. But it's a good reminder that sometimes a 'simple' search isn't the answer to everything.

Once you've had a look at some of those travel policies from the general search, go to one of the trade magazines: *Business Travel News* or *Buying Business Travel* for example. Now search for corporate travel policy on their sites and come back to answer the following question.

(1) What is the dominating opinion in the articles you've found on travel policy? Why do you think this is so?

_____

_____

_____

_____

_____

_____

_____

_____

_____

_____

_____

_____

_____

_____

Case Study Analysis

Let's look at one of the core challenges with travel policy: traveller engagement; in other words, making sure employees are compliant to set guidelines and mandates. We live in a world that's flooding us with information. Wherever we turn there are things trying to capture our attention and it's becoming increasingly difficult to stay focused on one thing. So what can be done?

The obvious solution is communication. Yet, communication can take many shapes and forms. "What is right?" and "what will work?" are some questions travel managers have to think about. And the answers aren't the same for everyone. Travel policy is written by and for a company with its own unique culture. It might be heavily mandated, meaning travellers have to obey the rules or be prepared to face a warning letter that could result in termination of employment. On the other end of the spectrum, travel policy might only be regarded as guidelines to give employees direction on what to do.

While the question of which communication style to adopt may vary, the outcome is the same across the board: driving traveller engagement and, ultimately, ownership. Why? That's the reason: the why. Today, and for the past few years, we've been learning to question things. We're not blindly following whatever we're told to do, but thinking for ourselves whether it makes sense to follow – or if there might be a better way to reach the same goal. In short, we thrive on explanations! They don't need to be lengthy, but if employees understand the reasons for travel policy compliance, they're much more likely to adhere to it.

For travel managers that means sharing the reasons for travel policy almost more importantly than sharing the policy itself. Let's look at a common problem travel managers have to deal with: an employee comes to the travel manager to say, "I found the London to New York flight much cheaper on the internet than on the online booking tool we're told to use". The employee wants to be a 'good citizen' and save company money, not realising that the deal he booked comes with a plethora of terms and conditions. If all goes well, the employee travels on the booked date and (if he's really lucky) he'll be reimbursed for the flight.

But what if it doesn't go well? What if the employee needs to change the date of the flight because a meeting has changed? He may find that with the ticket he booked, he cannot make any changes. He calls the TMC to help him, but they don't have access to this booking because it wasn't made through company channels. In the end he has to cancel the flight completely, forfeiting the money paid, and make a completely new booking. The cost is now much higher to the company – even if the employee's intentions were good.

Had the travel manager communicated and / or explained why travel policy is needed, the employee might not have looked (and booked) on the internet at all. Negotiated rates often have much better terms and conditions, like a free date change and / or cancellation.

Communication is key to help employees understand and comply with travel policy. Whichever shape it takes to get the message across, it helps with engagement and ownership. Travellers become convinced it's the right thing to book 'in policy' and start talking about it to others in the company. And word-of-mouth is still the best promotion one could wish for.

(1) How would you try to engage travellers?

_____

_____

_____

_____

_____

_____

_____

_____

_____

_____

_____

_____

_____

_____

_____

_____

_____

_____

_____

_____

_____

(2) What are the most important parts of a travel policy to ensure engagement?

_____

_____

_____

_____

_____

_____

_____

_____

_____

_____

_____

_____

_____

_____

_____

_____

_____

_____

_____

_____

_____

(3) In what way could you ensure travellers have a sense of ownership?

Sourcing

We've just talked about the importance of complying with policy and explaining the reasons to travellers. Sourcing travel suppliers plays a big part in this, as it's with negotiated contracts that travel managers ensure special terms, conditions and fares.

Usually, sourcing refers to procurement processes of goods and services. That means deals are made on a certain scope of order. In corporate travel you also need to know how to source, creating requests for proposals (RFPs), evaluating and contracting. Furthermore, there are differences in sourcing depending on which suppliers you want to integrate, so we distinguish some practices between air and hotel.

Critical Thinking

Generally, in business, sourcing refers to various procurement processes mainly split between strategic and global sourcing. Since corporate travel management sometimes reports to the procurement department, it's good idea to have some understanding of what sourcing means for them.

(1) What's the difference between general business sourcing and sourcing for corporate travel?

_____

_____

_____

_____

_____

_____

_____

_____

_____

_____

_____

(2) Why is sourcing important for corporate travel?

_____

_____

_____

_____

_____

_____

_____

_____

_____

_____

_____

_____

_____

_____

_____

_____

_____

_____

_____

(3) What's the difference between air and hotel sourcing?

_____

_____

_____

_____

_____

_____

_____

_____

_____

_____

_____

_____

_____

_____

_____

_____

_____

_____

_____

_____

_____

Research

As stated in the introduction, there are differences between air and hotel sourcing. Their offering is similar (a space to stay for some time), but it's also vastly different. There are many airlines across the world, but their numbers don't come close to the amount of hotels on the planet. We look more closely at hotel sourcing in the case study.

For this research, please go online to find Scott Gillespie's blogpost (gillespie411.wordpress.com). Once you're on the site, search for airline sourcing. There are a couple of posts that give you a good idea what it means to source, what data is needed and what is currently happening in the field. Once you've read the information, answer this question:

(1) How is the industry trying to make processes for airline contracting more efficient?

_____

_____

_____

_____

_____

_____

_____

_____

_____

_____

_____

_____

_____

Case Study Analysis

As mentioned, hotel sourcing can be very complex. There are a number of hotels in any given location: some are independent, some are chains, some are franchises. Sourcing contracts can be valid for a chain, or (more often) for a particular brand within that chain. Sourcing might be done at market level (in a certain city, destination or location), or at country, regional and even global level.

These few lines already show how fragmented the hotel space is. In the end, it often comes down to who knows whom and which hotels are closest to the office or meeting spaces usually frequented by corporate travellers.

The big challenge is getting correct information for benchmarking and analysis. That's why the request for proposal (RFP) was created: to have a standardised way to look at hotel services (and be able to compare them with others). However, the traditional hotel RFP is a very lengthy document to fill out, and some suppliers question the value of it. Creating and responding to an RFP is time consuming, and it's not always clear if the time spent is going to be rewarded in the end.

But it's not only the hotels that are struggling with filling out the information – it's also the travel managers. They have to merge collected data and analyse it to understand which hotels are best suited to their needs. As that information is often incomplete or submitted in different documents than those asked for, this is not an easy task.

There's a whole lot of choice in the market: different hotel categories, prices, locations, amenities and many other things (like concierge or room services). There's also the added difficulty that different countries have different star-ratings (or none at all). And with all these choices it gets increasingly difficult to compare the right hotels. Limiting the search to 'upscale' hotels (in the US or UK these would be three to four star properties) might leave off independent or luxury hotels that are willing to offer a very good rate for the right client.

A possible solution could be a map-based tool that shows relevant properties based on a selection of filters. The travel manager could at a glance see the hotels already on the programme in relation to the office address (or multiple meeting locations). She could also see other hotels in the same location range and get an average price to see if they might be interesting for inclusion.

The future for such a tool lies also with traveller engagement, as feedback from (recent) stays could be integrated in the tool and would add value to the travel manager. However, that implies that the tool needs access to multiple clients (masked data, of course!) to truly enrich the experience for travel managers across the globe.

(1) Why is hotel sourcing so difficult for travel managers?

_____

_____

_____

_____

_____

_____

_____

_____

_____

_____

_____

_____

_____

_____

_____

_____

_____

_____

_____

_____

_____

(2) How would you ensure that the best hotels (in terms of price, service and location) make it onto the corporate travel programme?

_____

_____

_____

_____

_____

_____

_____

_____

_____

_____

_____

_____

_____

_____

_____

_____

_____

_____

_____

_____

_____

(3) How would you ensure the hotels on the programme are also the ones booked by the travellers?

_____

_____

_____

_____

_____

_____

_____

_____

_____

_____

_____

_____

_____

_____

_____

_____

_____

_____

_____

Operations

The operations of a travel programme are quite different from the general use of the word in other industries. Nonetheless, travel managers do look after the efficient running of processes: bookings, cancellations, amendments, disruption, communications, expenses – the list just goes on and on. And it's their job to make sure everything is going smoothly or, if not, jump in and get things back on track.

Next is managing the big picture. Similar to travel policy and sourcing, there are other categories a travel manager needs to work in, like travel risk management, reporting and corporate social responsibility (CSR).

Critical Thinking

With all the wok you've been doing, you're well equipped to answer the following questions. Remember that you also have the corresponding chapter in the *Corporate Travel: Hiding In Plain Sight* if you want more information on any of this.

(1) What are daily operations travel managers are confronted with?

_____

_____

_____

_____

_____

_____

_____

_____

_____

_____

_____

(2) What are some of the annual operations in corporate travel?

_____

_____

_____

_____

_____

_____

_____

_____

_____

_____

_____

_____

_____

_____

_____

_____

_____

_____

_____

_____

_____

_____

(3) If you were a travel manager, what would be your biggest challenge?

_____

_____

_____

_____

_____

_____

_____

_____

_____

_____

_____

_____

_____

_____

_____

_____

_____

_____

_____

_____

_____

Research

Let's have some fun with this research task – and further your knowledge while we're at it. Go online (as usual) and search for 'corporate travel manager' jobs. You can choose a job site you're familiar with or just go to reed.co.uk to start off. Select a header that looks appealing to you and read through the advert. You might want to check one or two different postings to get a feel for the skills and requirements necessary for the job.

When you're done (you might have even applied for a job while at it!) come back here and answer the following question:

(1) What skills does a travel manager need today?

_____

_____

_____

_____

_____

_____

_____

_____

_____

_____

_____

_____

_____

Case Study Analysis

Corporate Social Responsibility, or rather CSR, is the topic for this case study. It's a topic that's been discussed in many industries and is often used to boost a company's reputation. There are many great initiatives coming from companies' CSR programmes and one shouldn't discount those as 'just' a marketing tactic.

One of the topics within CSR under constant scrutiny is CO_2 emissions. You're well aware, I'm sure, that these are very high for air travel – especially in business class. And so it's once more down to travel managers to run initiatives to keep CO_2 emissions in check.

What's the challenge? Travel managers want to do their bit for the environment. When surveying them, CSR initiatives are often high up on the agenda. Yet, too often they fall off the radar again when it's time to take action: cost savings and travel risk management have precedence over CSR. And a lot of resources are needed to actually make a difference without affecting the business.

Yet CSR has become more important in 2015 with important changes to global emissions signed during the United Nations Climate Change Conference in Paris. Overall, 2015 was a year driving CSR on the corporate agenda and companies are now charged with finding ways to do their bit.

Enter the travel manager. With all the other things going on, there's hardly time to think about CSR initiatives as well. But how about combining some things to drive results in more than one category? Within the corporate travel trends section, we discussed behavioural economics and the role they can have in the industry. This can also be applied to CSR.

1. Using behavioural economic messaging at point of planning or purchase to alert the traveller about:

   a. CO2 emissions created by the trip
   b. Alternative travel option (if possible)
   c. Optional participation in initiative to balance CO2 emission (like planting a tree)

2. Using gamification as company-wide practice to compete for lowering CO2 emissions by:

   a. Targeting travel-heavy departments
   b. Raising awareness for the campaign on intra-company channels
   c. Recognise winners and share how they did it

Using behavioural economics helps with traveller engagement. CSR is a particularly good topic to get employee buy-in because everyone wants to save the planet. The initiative could also boost the reputation of the travel manager (or travel department). Using gamification helps not only with traveller engagement, but also with policy compliance. Booking through corporate channels means less waste, which can equal fewer CO2 emissions.

(1) Why is CSR important for corporate travel?

_____

_____

_____

_____

_____

_____

_____

_____

_____

_____

_____

_____

_____

_____

_____

_____

_____

_____

_____

_____

_____

(2) What initiatives would you want to create to support CSR goals overall?

_____

_____

_____

_____

_____

_____

_____

_____

_____

_____

_____

_____

_____

_____

_____

_____

_____

_____

_____

_____

(3) How would you raise awareness for CSR?

_____

_____

_____

_____

_____

_____

_____

_____

_____

_____

_____

_____

_____

_____

_____

_____

_____

_____

_____

_____

Things To Remember

➤ Travel policy sets out rules and regulations by which employees must comply when traveling. This isn't only important for their safety, but also to make negotiations work.

➤ Creating policy with input from many stakeholders helps create ownership within the company.

➤ Sourcing suppliers and negotiating prices is much more complex in travel than it is for other categories, such as stationery. Mostly because travel managers cannot guarantee the scope of the order.

➤ Operations in travel management range from demand and behaviour management to corporate social responsibility (CSR) and depend on whether a programme is managed locally, regionally or globally.

➤ On a normal day, a travel manager might deal with a volcano eruption, reporting tools and supplier visits. Never a dull moment.

The Trip Life Cycle

The world is a book and those who do not
travel read only one page.

~ St. Augustine

Checklist

By the end of this part you'll be able to:

✓ Recognise the differences between trip life cycles for leisure and corporate travellers.

✓ Understand the different components of the life cycle, like planning, booking, on the go and follow up.

✓ Appreciate how the travel programme impacts the traveller and protects their wellbeing.

Introduction

Finally, it's time to talk about the traveller! But it still has a lot to do with the travel manager, suppliers, technology and all the other good things already discussed. Only now we're considering how the traveller fits in with corporate travel management. And that means, looking at it from the traveller's point of view.

The trip life cycle, meaning the moment from planning a trip until returning and filing expenses, is the last part of this workbook. And so it starts with an overview of the trip life cycle of a leisure traveller. Once you've reminded yourself of the different stages, we look at a trip life cycle for corporate travel in particular. This gives further insights into the interaction between traveller and travel managers. And these are most apparent in the different stages: planning and booking, on the go, and follow-up.

Lastly, business intelligence and data have already been talked about a little throughout this workbook, but it's an important area for travel managers. So it's only fitting that this topic concludes this book. We have a look at how travel managers use on-trip data to make better decisions for the travel programme in the future. There's a case study on mobile apps and how they are going to add more data streams that will help to reveal total trip spend – the Holy Grail for travel managers.

About Life Cycles

Life cycles are used throughout the (business) world to illustrate the different stages an individual or a product (or service) goes through. We call them cycles because the stages are recurring continuously. The four seasons are, in a way, nature's annual life cycle – new growth in spring, bloom in summer, shutting down of the system in autumn and deep slumber in winter.

The point is that all stages depend on one another. None can exist if the others haven't been completed. And that's how it is for travel too, whether it's leisure trips or corporate travel management. The key differences are in the introduction of complexities. The trip life cycle in a business to consumer (B2C) environment is naturally less complex than adding in a third dimension via the travel manager.

Critical Thinking

The trip life cycle for the leisure traveller concentrates on their awareness of new destinations (and their own feeling of being ready for another holiday). For corporate travellers, the awareness is a new business opportunity or meeting request. It might even often be coupled with the feeling of not wanting to travel yet again.

(1) Aside from the awareness stage, what other differences do you see between leisure and corporate trip life cycles?

_____

_____

_____

_____

_____

_____

_____

_____

_____

_____

(2) Why is the corporate travel life cycle more complex than the leisure one?

_____

_____

_____

_____

_____

_____

_____

_____

_____

_____

_____

_____

_____

_____

_____

_____

_____

_____

_____

(3) What do you consider the most important stage of the corporate travel life cycle?

_____

_____

_____

_____

_____

_____

_____

_____

_____

_____

_____

_____

_____

_____

_____

_____

_____

_____

Research

Let's take it one step further and have a look at the overall travel management cycle. You can find an illustration in a BCD white paper called 'Traveler Management'. Look this up online and see the different stages. Some are things the travel manager has to do, while others apply to the travellers themselves.

The paper was written to highlight one of the trends: personalisation. Corporate travel management is going further and further towards traveller management. Meaning travellers are taken into account for all the different stages to ensure their productivity on the road, but also their wellbeing.

(1) In your opinion, is the shift towards traveller centricity and personalisation necessary for successful corporate travel management? Why?

_____

_____

_____

_____

_____

_____

_____

_____

_____

_____

_____

_____

_____

_____

Case Study Analysis

In reality, the corporate travel life cycle often doesn't feel like a cycle at all. More like a linear process with a beginning and an end. Travellers often feel left out of the policy: while they have to adhere to it, they have very little chance to share their opinions and thoughts for input.

The challenge for every travel manager is listening to travellers. That's not only a challenge for them, but for most of us human beings. Listening is an art form, especially when you want to hear the fine nuances or the very quiet tones. And let's be honest: we generally only give feedback when something goes wrong. When things are going as planned, we take them for granted; not spending a second thought on how well everything worked out (aside from patting our own back for very good planning).

When we do receive feedback it's mostly bad and often shared very loudly. If you think of a traditional walk-in travel agency, and a customer comes in after a trip to complain about something or other, you can be sure everyone in the room hears him. Today, the sharing is done through social media channels. Frustration is shared and quickly goes viral – an unfortunate situation for the supplier who is now perceived to give bad service.

Back to our corporate travellers and their options to share feedback. Many TMCs today offer surveys to their corporate clients. These might be geared towards the travel managers, to find out how satisfied they are with the support and services they receive, and they're geared towards travellers at the point of return, to find out about one specific element of the trip or the overall experience. Because we grapple with so many things to do, these surveys tend to be very short (up to three questions).

It's because of this that travel managers still struggle to get valuable input for their policies: answering three questions about a trip (including flight, airport transfer, hotel, taxi, public transportation, train, another hotel, more ground transportation and finally another flight) is hardly informative enough to give travel managers something to work with. However, it does give a good trend indication of whether, in general, the policy works – or not.

The solution might be to send out longer surveys, including all the elements used during the trip and asking the traveller to fill out a rating based on the services received. But participation is very likely going to be low. What's going to be more useful in the longer term are even shorter polls: one question surveys at point of engagement. This is (and will be) possible through, for example, GPS technology. The survey tool would automatically send a poll to the traveller's smartphone 30 minutes after arrival at hotel with a question about the check-in experience.

This is starting to be used more and more in business as well as in private: think of how we can now set our own reminders based on location. However, data security must be in place to protect personal data as well as company data for travellers on the road.

Obtaining this real-time information will be invaluable for travel managers who can tweak travel policy to ensure travellers' needs are met and company standards are adhered to. It'll also come in useful during negotiations with suppliers.

(1) Why is feedback so important to corporate travel management?

_____

_____

_____

_____

_____

_____

_____

_____

_____

_____

_____

_____

_____

_____

_____

_____

_____

_____

_____

_____

_____

_____

(2) Why do you think is it so difficult to get feedback?

_____

_____

_____

_____

_____

_____

_____

_____

_____

_____

_____

_____

_____

_____

_____

_____

_____

_____

(3) What other options can you think of to 'close the loop' and continue the cycle?

_____

_____

_____

_____

_____

_____

_____

_____

_____

_____

_____

_____

_____

_____

_____

_____

_____

_____

_____

_____

Planning & Booking

Planning a trip is different from the leisure side, as just discussed, because the reason to travel is business. Planning, therefore, focuses on convenience of options, proximity of hotels to meeting facilities and making the most of the time abroad.

However, there's another side to planning often overlooked for leisure trips: travel risk management. Companies have to comply with duty of care regulations and so travellers should fit some briefing or information (always depending on the destination) into their planning stage.

Critical Thinking

There are several ways to go about booking a trip, often depending on the complexities of the journey. Online booking tools, call centre agents and newly emerging options through mobile apps. As long as booking through corporate channels, the traveller is sure to have someone they can call 24/7 if something were to go wrong. A luxury few leisure travellers have.

(1) How do corporate travellers plan their trips?

_____

_____

_____

_____

_____

_____

_____

_____

_____

_____

_____

_____

_____

(2) Why is travel risk management so important in corporate travel?

(3) What steps could you take to ensure employees book via corporate channels?

_____

_____

_____

_____

_____

_____

_____

_____

_____

_____

_____

_____

_____

_____

_____

_____

_____

_____

_____

Research

You already worked on building a travel risk management policy with an earlier case study. But every policy needs to be read, understood and acted upon. During the planning stage, the traveller should receive a destination briefing. This document gives guidance on what (not) to do and where to find help in case of an emergency.

Have a look at GeoReach's website online to see how they keep travellers (and people overall) safe. They're one of the providers that travel managers work with to ensure traveller safety. When you've had a good look, answer the following question:

(1) What new technology is GeoReach using to keep travellers safe? How does the travel manager benefit from their services?

_____

_____

_____

_____

_____

_____

_____

_____

_____

_____

_____

_____

_____

_____

Case Study Analysis

In the critical thinking part, you considered how corporate travellers plan their trips. Many companies have TMCs helping their employees with planning and booking. This can be done through call centres and agents for complex itineraries and online booking tools for the simpler 'there and back again' requests. Companies that don't have significant travel spend often opt for an online booking tool only.

This makes planning simple for the traveller, right? Yes, but temptation lies outside the corporate channels: the internet. You're well aware, of course, about the plethora of options to book travel. There are meta search engines making all components of your holiday bookable, and those that specialise on one segment. And because we like to compare offers, we look at different options. We're always happy to pick up a bargain!

Corporate travellers are also human and want to have the best hassle-free trip they can. So if they don't quite trust the options the online booking tool is suggesting, they might just jump onto a search engine and see if there are any alternatives out there. Often they're unsuccessful in finding better connections, BUT they're successful in finding better prices. It's with this information they come to the travel manager to brag about being able to find better deals. However, they often don't know what extras and conditions they would have had with the corporate negotiated deal.

While it's somewhat annoying for travel managers to be 'caught-out' like that, there's an even more important reason why employees should stick to corporate channels: time. Employees waste two to three hours to scour the internet for best travel options: time that should be spent on the job they were employed to do.

A solution to this problem is already being used across many companies: trip approval. That means the traveller has to get approval from their line manager for a trip – prior to booking, but post planning. For example, the employee plans a trip from London to New York for an internal meeting. She sends a travel request to the TMC with the dates and times she needs to be there. After some time, she receives an email with the travel options and prices for the trip. She selects one option and copies in her line manager to approve the cost and trip for the travel department.

It's a lengthy process and comes with risks: because travel isn't booked immediately, prices might change until approval is obtained. Or flights might become unavailable. That's why there's a trend to use trip approval automation with the online booking tool. Once the employee selects their preferred option the trip is booked while simultaneously, an email is sent to the line manager alerting him of the upcoming trip. There's still time to stop the process, but if the trip is approved, the reservation is already confirmed.

But how does that help with travellers sticking to the booking tool or their agents? It is one thing to check flights and hotels on the internet, but quite another to have the courage to ask your line manager's approval for such an option. When the employee knows that her line manager gets a copy of the booking and has to approve it, chances are much higher she'll stick to the corporate channels.

(1) Why are travellers searching the internet for travel options?

_____

_____

_____

_____

_____

_____

_____

_____

_____

_____

_____

_____

_____

_____

_____

_____

_____

_____

_____

_____

(2) What is the purpose of the trip approval?

_____

_____

_____

_____

_____

_____

_____

_____

_____

_____

_____

_____

_____

_____

_____

_____

_____

_____

_____

_____

(3) Do you think trip approval is necessary for corporate travel? Why?

_____

_____

_____

_____

_____

_____

_____

_____

_____

_____

_____

_____

_____

_____

_____

_____

_____

_____

_____

_____

On the Go

Now the traveller is good to go. Travel starts and for many of the road warriors out there, they might heave a sigh of relief to finally be outside the grasp of the travel manager – free to do as they please. Or so they hope. And even as little as five years ago they would have been right.

Times are changing, however, and the smartphone has done its best to enter not only into different industries, but most importantly, into our personal lives. It's unthinkable not to be connected, and if there's an issue with internet connectivity people feel anxious about missing out on something.

Corporate travellers are no exception and this could very well be their 'Achilles' heel'. While traditionally, people had one mobile for work and one for personal use, the trend today is BYOD – bring your own device. This holds true for mobile phones and, increasingly, laptops as well.

Critical Thinking

Communications can make a travel programme work. On the flip side, lack of communication or too much 'spamming' can also break a travel programme and disengage travellers.

(1) What are benefits of constant availability through smartphones while on the road?

_____

_____

_____

_____

_____

_____

_____

_____

_____

_____

_____

(2) What are potential disadvantages of availability for the traveller?

_____

_____

_____

_____

_____

_____

_____

_____

_____

_____

_____

_____

_____

_____

_____

_____

_____

_____

_____

_____

_____

_____

(3) How do you see the current BYOD trend developing in the next five years?

_____

_____

_____

_____

_____

_____

_____

_____

_____

_____

_____

_____

_____

_____

_____

_____

_____

_____

_____

_____

Research

You've just spent some time thinking about communications, as well as the advantages and disadvantages of being constantly online and available. There's one option to consider in order not to give too little or too much information: employing a 'push and pull strategy'.

This strategy enables the travel manager to push important information out to travellers on the go. At the same time, further information (so-called 'nice to know') can be made easily accessible from a smartphone device.

Head online and search for push and pull strategy. Then come back here and answer the following question:

(1) How can you ensure the right information is pushed out to travellers? What makes information important enough to be pushed?

_____

_____

_____

_____

_____

_____

_____

_____

_____

_____

_____

_____

_____

_____

_____

_____

Case Study Analysis

Talking about the traveller and the part they play in a corporate travel programme always seems to go hand-in-hand with talking about compliance and costs. This case study is no exception as we look at ancillary services (and fees) that often tempt travellers on the road.

We all know the scenario: we arrive at the airport, tired and possibly annoyed because of traffic, and the check-in attendant informs us that only middle seats are now available in the rear of the aircraft. However, there is a possibility to upgrade to premium economy or even business class. It's tempting.

Many ancillary services are needed for a corporate traveller and companies do pay for them. However, a study by Business Travel News from 2012 showed a big discrepancy between what people thought they could expense and what companies were actually happy to expense (and it was mostly in favour for travellers!).

So aside from spending more money than they should, why is there a problem with ancillary fees? There are in fact several challenges:

- Communication: ensuring travellers know what they can and can't expense.
- Transparency: ensuring travellers don't pay double for what might be included in negotiated rates.
- Data: knowing how much is spent on one trip and what for.

We've already talked about the importance of communication and different ways of engaging with travellers at some length through this book (and you've given it much more thought as well). The data topic and importance of business intelligence to run a successful and efficient travel programme is covered in the next case study.

Transparency is the one we focus on here. During planning and booking we've already touched upon the importance on staying within corporate channels. You also know that often travellers are unaware of the benefits of booking negotiated deals. But you might not be aware that aside from easy cancellation or date changes, suppliers often negotiate ancillaries as well.

The industry (in part) is looking forward to new distribution capabilities (NDC) of the GDSs across the globe. These should be able to showcase ancillary services and allow like-for-like comparison on the screen. Note that, currently, the traveller or agent would have to look at the individual supplier websites to find out what is (or isn't) included. Once the information is loaded in the GDS, it is also available in the online booking tools. Travellers should then be able, at a glance, to see what they get for their money.

(1) What are ancillary services?

_____

_____

_____

_____

_____

_____

_____

_____

_____

_____

_____

_____

_____

_____

_____

_____

_____

_____

_____

_____

_____

(2) How can you ensure travellers know which ancillary services are already part of negotiated deals?

_____

_____

_____

_____

_____

_____

_____

_____

_____

_____

_____

_____

_____

_____

_____

_____

_____

_____

_____

_____

_____

(3) Would you speak with suppliers to tackle ancillary spending of your travellers? How would you go about it?

_____

_____

_____

_____

_____

_____

_____

_____

_____

_____

_____

_____

_____

_____

_____

_____

_____

Follow-Up

You might think that once the traveller is back from her trip that's it. Maybe there are some pictures to post or order prints of – reminders of a good time. But that's not the case in corporate travel, I'm afraid. There are reminders (and often of a good time, too) but they're in the form of carefully collected receipts.

This collection might sit for some time before employees can muster up the strength to tackle the admin involved. But back under the watchful eye of the travel manager, that is, back in the office, there's little time to dawdle.

Next to the expenses, there's feedback to give about the services used and whether everything was as expected. Feedback is a necessary tool for travel managers to have 'ammunition' for negotiations, but it should also inform and link into travel policy.

Critical Thinking

For the travel manager, it's time to collect data: not only traveller feedback, but also information from different sources. This can be booking details, credit card statements and supplier reports.

(1) What questions would you ask a traveller who just returned from a business trip?

_____

_____

_____

_____

_____

_____

_____

_____

_____

_____

(2) Why, in your opinion, is expense management important for corporate travel?

_____

_____

_____

_____

_____

_____

_____

_____

_____

_____

_____

_____

_____

_____

_____

_____

_____

_____

_____

_____

_____

(3) How can the travel manager ensure they have access to all necessary data?

_____

_____

_____

_____

_____

_____

_____

_____

_____

_____

_____

_____

_____

_____

_____

_____

_____

_____

_____

_____

_____

Research

We've just raised the question regarding the importance of expense management. In corporate travel it is a very important part of the whole picture. It ties in with another trend: end-to-end travel management. It means giving the traveller a seamless and user-friendly approach to the complete trip cycle – including the integration of payments and expense reporting.

Have a look online to find out more about end-to-end in corporate travel. There are some studies from Amadeus, Concur and BCD Travel you might find worthwhile. Then answer the following question:

(1) What is meant by the 'end-to-end' process in corporate travel? How does this impact expense management?

_____

_____

_____

_____

_____

_____

_____

_____

_____

_____

_____

_____

_____

_____

Case Study Analysis

Information is key. Decision-making relies on quality information and business intelligence. That's true for all industries and all people – and also for corporate travel management. It's therefore surprising that reporting and analysis are still mainly done on Excel spreadsheets.

While big data was hailed as the answer to all data questions starting (for corporate travel) in 2013, it seems that expectations were too high and deliverables a let-down.

The first challenge is data accessibility and the question 'who actually owns the data?'. Is it the company making a booking? The company facilitating the booking? Or the company carrying out the booking? In the end, all of them have access to data and need to keep to standards to ensure data safety.

The next challenge is the question, 'Who is going to analyse the data?'. This could be the client or the TMC (most of the time). But thinking back to the first challenge: how does the TMC get access to all the data? This is where it starts to get a little messy. For a true travel spend picture, multiple data sources are needed:

- Booking data (prior to traveling)
- Transaction data (post traveling)
- Booking and transaction data of bookings made via another agency
- Booking and transaction data for maverick bookings (outside corporate channels)
- Supplier data (to match with transaction data)
- Credit card data
- Expense data

Back to the analysis: with so many data sources, it's immediately apparent that a specialist would probably be the best solution to look at this. But services of that kind are expensive and customised. So TMCs have been working to find basic off-the-shelf solutions to help travel managers with their data mire.

So-called third party data integration services function as a nexus to merge and standardise data to specifications. This is then loaded into the TMCs analytics tool and travel managers have a pretty dashboard to see where their budget is being spent. But it's early days yet, and there are many things we hope to see in the industry soon, like predictive and prescriptive analytics.

One last thought on data: why does it all take such long time to develop? Remember that the industry has been built on a structured data warehouse, essentially. Today, data is much more agile and flexible and can be 'called' by different computer programmes. Those same programmes struggle with structured data and in effect the (corporate) travel industry has been investing heavily to move to a level playing field.

(1) What are the difficulties currently hampering efforts to analyse data?

_____

_____

_____

_____

_____

_____

_____

_____

_____

_____

_____

_____

_____

_____

_____

_____

_____

_____

_____

_____

_____

(2) What are the benefits of third party data integration?

_____

_____

_____

_____

_____

_____

_____

_____

_____

_____

_____

_____

_____

_____

_____

_____

_____

_____

_____

(3) How would you use business intelligence to improve your travel programme?

_____

_____

_____

_____

_____

_____

_____

_____

_____

_____

_____

_____

_____

_____

_____

_____

_____

_____

_____

_____

Things to Remember

➤ Life cycles are often used in marketing to determine the phases of a product over time. In corporate travel, the trip life cycle does this too. Crucially, the follow up phase directly feeds into policy and planning to make this a true cycle.

➤ Planning and booking a trip through corporate channels should be quick, easy and efficient so that as little time as possible is lost searching different options. However, in practice that's not often the case.

➤ Corporate travellers on the go face different challenges to their leisure counterparts. And what's more, they have to justify their actions and payments to the company.

➤ Following up on a trip means doing expenses, which can be time consuming, especially if done with hard copy receipts. But it also means that the travel manager can find out how satisfied the traveller was, and what worked and what didn't.

➤ Lastly, and to loop back to the cycle, business intelligence provides the backbone of the industry. With the information collected from travellers and through different data sources, travel programmes become better and more user friendly over time.

Glossary of Terms & Abbreviations

Here's a list of corporate travel jargon and abbreviations to help you through the book, and possibly in real life as well.

Americas

Geographical region comprising North America (often called 'NORAM') and South America (somewhat confusingly called LATAM most often). Note that it's dependent on the company whether Mexico is counted towards north or south.

Asia Pacific (APAC)

Geographical region comprising Asia and Southwest Pacific (Australia, New Zealand). This region is also known as APAC, and there are some companies splitting Asia from Southwest Pacific as their booking behaviour and programme maturity are quite different.

Application programming interface (API)

This is a facilitator for different software programmes to interact. It's important in corporate travel to connect different booking sources, profile information and other (third party) content.

Association for Corporate Travel Executives (ACTE)

One of the global associations, particularly renowned for their efforts in educating the industry. They have several annual conferences across the world and many more local events and web-based trainings.

Average daily rate (ADR)

The ADR refers to either hotel or car rental rates. It's calculated by dividing the actual daily room revenue with the total number of rooms sold.

Average ticket price (ATP)

The ATP refers to airfares. It's a key metric to look at airfare trends. Take this with a pinch of salt as it becomes distorted the larger the area is that the ATP refers to (e.g. an ATP for the route of London-New York in economy class is very helpful because it's specific; a global ATP holds almost no value as too many variables are thrown into one pot.

Best available rate (BAR)

The BAR refers to the best non-negotiated rate on the day at the point of booking. This can include special rates that have to be pre-paid.

Blackout dates

These are dates during which hotels are not bound by the negotiated rates – provided they have been shared during the negotiations. For example, if the city hosts a big conference, hotels might apply blackout dates as demand will be high.

Business Travel News (BTN)

One of the media publications focusing on business and corporate travel. They're especially famous for the Corporate Travel Index and Fortune 100 company lists they publish annually.

Buying Business Travel

Another media outlet focusing mainly on the UK market and hosting great debate events together with ACTE (see below).

Corporate rates

Rates that companies negotiate together with the supplier; note that every company has their own corporate rates with suppliers.

Corporate social responsibility (CSR)

Corporations are increasingly urged to take on social responsibility. Often this is done through engagements with the local community. In corporate travel, CO_2 tracking and supporting projects or charities to combat emissions are one way to show responsibility.

Corporate travel management (CTM)

The managing of corporate travel, encompassing day-to-day operations, negotiations, duty of care and travel risk management on behalf of a company. Often in-house travel managers (see below) are supported by external travel management companies (see below).

Data consolidation

Within corporate travel, data consolidation refers to bringing different data sources together. These are usually booking and transaction data, supplier data and also payment and expense data; all of which is used for business intelligence and informed decision-making.

Distribution channel

This is the process of how the suppliers get their products to the travellers. The traditional distribution channel for corporate travel is the global distribution system (see below), though there are online alternatives through brokers as well as direct.

Dynamic pricing

In corporate travel, dynamic pricing offers an alternative to negotiated rates (especially for hotels). Prices are driven by the market and by demand, so they can vary from low in off-peak season to high when all rooms in a city are needed (for example, during a congress).

EMEA

Geographical region comprising Europe, Middle East and Africa. There's a shift in the industry to separate Europe from Middle East and Africa as the latter two are becoming more important economically – this is likely to continue, meaning Middle East and Africa will become distinct regions as well.

Expense management system

An all-important tool for travellers to be reimbursed after travel, the expense management system offers a range of features, including reporting, approving and paying expenses on an online platform.

Geo-coding

This is the ability to use coordinates, that is, degrees of latitude and longitude, for finding specific locations. It's also becoming increasingly popular with hotels to match property names and addresses for billing and reporting purposes.

Geo-fencing

Geo-fencing refers to the ability to track travellers in high-risk destinations. By using GPS signals (mostly), an alarm is raised when the traveller moves outside of predefined areas.

Global Business Travel Association (GBTA)

The other global association helping the corporate travel industry grow. Their members are travel managers and suppliers, sharing opinions and information to find best processes for the industry.

Global Distribution System (GDS)

There are several GDSs available around the world that connect supplier inventory with booking agents. Amadeus is particularly well-established in Europe, while Sabre has a stronghold in North America. Travelport is an important GDS in Asia.

Hub

An airport offering long-distance (often international) flights and many short-distance 'feeder' services is called a hub.

International Air Transport Association (IATA)

An important body, not only for corporate, but for all travel, IATA establishes standard practices and is also the governing body for international air-travel rules. Furthermore, they accredit travel agents, making the agency able to book through the GDSs and collect commissions for their bookings.

IMEX

A Frankfurt-based convention for meeting suppliers, featuring a hosted-buyer programme. Individuals and companies arranging meetings are invited free of charge to attend (including travel arrangements). In return, they have to schedule meetings with suppliers and other exhibitors.

Institute of Travel and Meetings (ITM)

This is one of the local associations operating in the UK Similarly to their global counterparts, they put on a range of localised events for travel managers and suppliers to exchange information and learn about the industry.

Itinerary

A chronological record of a traveller's trip, including all information about booked services, like flight information, hotel, car-rental and any other pre-booked items.

Key performance indicator (KPI)

Travel managers set targets for the travel programme and monitor these by using key performance indicators. They often include advance booking time, economy class ratio and online booking behaviour as well as many more programme-specific ones.

Lowest logical airfare

Corporate travellers are advised to use lowest logical airfares, and what is considered logical is determined by travel policy. For example, there might be cheaper flight options, though due to stopover connections, these might not be 'logical' for the company.

Managed travel

This means travel is actively and professionally managed within a corporation. It generally also means travel policy is in place and rates are negotiated with suppliers.

MICE

An industry abbreviation for meetings, incentives, conferences and exhibitions (or events in some cases).

Negotiated rate

This term is especially important for bookings on the GDS, as the client's code is needed to access negotiated rates agreed upon with the supplier.

Online booking tool (OBT)

As the name suggests, this is a tool for travellers (or their admin/agent) to use for booking travel. It's often customised for big corporations and gives the traveller access to preferred suppliers and rates. Using an OBT is time-efficient and costs less money compared to calling an agent on the phone (which is why this is an important KPI to track).

Online Travel Agency (OTA)

In the corporate travel industry, online travel agencies are completely virtual and don't have walk-in services.

Per diem

A daily allowance for a city or country that the corporate traveller receives when travelling.

Preferred suppliers

These are the suppliers that corporations have negotiated deals with. Hence travel managers try to drive business to these products and services.

Pre-trip authorisation

A process prior to booking to obtain approval, usually from the line-manager, for the trip.

Profiles

In corporate travel this refers to profiles stored within a customised database in the GDS. These profiles contain traveller information, preferences and loyalty cards and mean traveller data is automatically copied into a booking.

Rack rate

The rate hotels publish for their room. This is often the highest rate available and is usually displayed at reception.

Red-eye flight

A term for late-night flight departures, arriving at the destination early in the morning. The term is most commonly used in North America for west- to east-coast travel.

Request for information (RFI)

Before the travel manager decides which suppliers to invite to bid for their business, he often sends out a request for information first, to be able to compare suppliers' services.

Request for proposal (RFP)

Once a general selection is made about which suppliers to invite, a request for proposal is sent out. This is a document asking detailed questions about products, services, duty of care, price and other items, and determines whether a supplier is going to become the preferred one with a company.

Revenue management

Also known as yield management, this is the practice of suppliers (mainly airlines, hotels and car-rental companies) of controlling inventory and supply to maximise occupancy and revenue.

Service level agreement (SLA)

Similar to KPIs, these measure the quality of services and make sure key suppliers are adhering to them. Assessment factors are, amongst others, response time to answer phone calls, policy enforcement and contract savings.

Skift

An online publication offering global travel-industry intelligence. While they're looking at travel overall, they often have interesting thought pieces on corporate travel as well.

Tnooz

Another publication focusing on technology in travel. They're often looking at the future and what's going to impact corporate travel.

Travel Management Company (TMC)

An intermediary company to support corporations with managing their travel programme. They traditionally book travel, like agencies, but also look after the many back-office needs of corporate travel, like duty of care requirements, negotiations, payments and many more.

Travel Manager

The person in charge of travel management at a company. This might be a single individual or a full team, depending on the size of the company.

Travel Risk Management

An essential part of travel management is managing risks on the road as well. This is often done using a third-party (specialist) provider.

Unmanaged travel

A term used for companies that don't travel enough to require a travel programme or policy in place. They often don't have negotiated deals in place and many book through online channels only.

Value added tax (VAT)

A tax imposed by many governments across the world on goods and services. This tax is often recoverable for corporations – even across borders.

World Travel and Tourism Council (WTTC)

An international organisation of travel-industry executives promoting travel and tourism worldwide. Its members come from the global business community as well as from governments.

World Travel Organization (WTO)

An organisation formed by the United Nations to promote responsible, sustainable and universally accessible tourism.

Further Reading

This is an excerpt of the bibliography of the book *Corporate Travel: Hiding in Plain Sight.* You might find this a good list of suggested further reading. Some of the sources also contain more case studies and other materials.

ACTE. (n.d.). *ACTE Global: Association of Corporate Travel Executives* . Retrieved September 17, 2015, from https://www.acte.org/about.htm

Advito. (2014). *Industry Forecast 2015*. Advito. Retrieved from http://www.advito.com/solutions/wp-advito-industry-forecast-2015/

Advito. (2015, July). *Advito*. Retrieved from Advito social community playbook: http://www.advito.com/solutions/advito-social-community-playbook/

Ariely, D. (2009). *Predictably Irrational*. Harper Collins.

BCD Travel. (2015). *BCD Travel - Travel Management*. Retrieved August 22, 2015, from http://www.bcdtravel.com/travel-services/travel-management/

BTN - Business Travel News. (2015). *BTN's 2015 Corporate Travel Index*. Northstar Media. Retrieved from http://www.businesstravelnews.com/Business-Travel-Research/BTN-s-2015-Corporate-Travel-Index/

BTN. (2014). *Corporate Travel 100*. Secaucus, NJ, USA: Northstar Travel Media.

BTN. (2015). *Business Travel News Handbook Glossary*. Retrieved August 22, 2015, from http://www.businesstravelnews.com/Handbook/Handbook.Terms.ashx?HL=tmc

Carlson Wagonlit Travel. (2015). *Business Travel*. Retrieved August 22, 2015, from http://www.carlsonwagonlit.com/en/global/business-travel/

Concur. (2015). *Expense Management Made Easy*. Retrieved September 18, 2015, from https://www.concur.co.uk/expense-management?icid=en_uk_home_expense

Davidson, R., & Cope, B. (2003). *Business Travel*. Harlow, England: Pearson Education Limited.

Forbes. (2015). *The World's Biggest Public Companies - Airlines*. Retrieved August 23, 2015, from http://www.forbes.com/global2000/list/#header:revenue_sortreverse:true_industry:Airline

GBT. (2015). *American Express - Global Business Travel*. Retrieved from 100 Years of Business Travel: https://www.amexglobalbusinesstravel.com/100thanniversary/files/GBT100_Milestones_1915-1955.jpg

GBTA. (2015). *About GBTA*. Retrieved September 17, 2015, from http://www.gbta.org/about/Pages/Default.aspx

Tribe, J. (2011). *The Economics of Recreation, Leisure and Tourism* (4 ed.). Oxford, Great Britain: Butterworth-Heinemann.

Unger, C. (2016). Corporate Travel: Hiding in Plain Sight. Createspace.

UNWTO. (2014). *Glossary of tourism terms*. Retrieved July 22, 2015, from https://s3-eu-west-1.amazonaws.com/staticunwto/Statistics/Glossary+of+terms.pdf

WTTC. (2015). *Travel and Tourism Economic Impact 2014 World*. World Travel & Tourism Council. Retrieved 2015, from http://www.wttc.org/-/media/files/reports/economic%20impact%20research/regional%20reports/world2014.pdf

Also by Claudia Unger